Benchmark Hunting
In
Yellowstone National Park

Thomas P. Bohannan

HAYDEN PUBLISHING
New Castle, Delaware

Published by: Hayden Publishing
New Castle, Delaware

Photographs and illustrations by the author unless otherwise noted.

Library of Congress Control Number: 2012936316
ISBN: 978-0-9854072-0-9 (Bound)
ISBN: 978-0-9854072-1-6 (E-Book)

Front Cover Photo: Albright Visitor Center, Yellowstone National Park. Inset is overhead view of benchmark PY0160, located on concrete pedestal in front of the Visitor Center.

Back Cover Photo: View of Fort Yellowstone and Mammoth Hot Springs from the Gardiner High Road, July 9, 2011. Bunsen Peak is in the background.

The discoveries narrated form an event of high public interest in the history of the United States, and have already been the subject of a legislative enactment. In consideration of the importance of the discoveries, and from a conviction this region will be a place of resort for visitors from all parts of the world, the Senate and House of Representatives, on March 1, 1872, passed an act withdrawing from settlement, occupancy, or sale, under the laws of the United States, the tract of land described, being in extent 55 by 65 miles, and which territory is dedicated and set apart as a great national park or pleasure ground for the benefit and enjoyment of the people.

~James Richardson

FOREWORD

Perhaps it's a modest overstatement, but the information provided in this book describes the physical realization of one of the most important parts of our nation's infrastructure. It is very safe to say that everything is about place. Everything happens somewhere and knowing the relationship of one place to another has always been of vital importance. This begs of the question, how do we know where everything is? We have a map or a chart. It may be paper or digital, in our hands, on a computer screen, or on a "smart" device. What makes the map accurate? Bench marks make maps and charts accurate.

Used in the generic sense, the term "bench marks" refers to permanent fixtures for which a very, very accurate height, commonly referenced to some definition of mean sea level and/or a horizontal position (latitude and longitude) have been determined. These markers usually consisting of a brass, bronze or aluminum marker imbedded in concrete or bed rock, scattered around Yellowstone and the rest of the country provide the foundation for ensuring the integrity of all forms of mapping and charting as well as providing a framework to understand changes in our landscape.

The first high accuracy survey, often called a geodetic survey, in Yellowstone was performed in 1923 under the direction of the U.S. Coast and Geodetic Survey (USC&GS), today called the National Geodetic Survey (NGS). Geodetic surveys are often painstakingly slow but result in the most accurate determination of height and position. Since then numerous surveys of Yellowstone have been conducted by several Federal and state agencies and research institutions using a variety of state of the art technology, most recently the Global Positioning System (GPS). Details of these various efforts are provided by the author. The bench marks left as a physical reference for these surveys serve as the starting points for practical day-to-day needs such as road and highway construction, building irrigation systems, housing subdivisions and building complexes. These same points also provide the basis for scientific investigations of the complex motions of the Earth's tectonic plates – a very active feature of Yellowstone.

The collection provided by Mr. Bohannan is a detailed inventory of many of the bench marks established as a result of these surveys. As you look for these markers (a process often called "recovery"), I hope you will take a few minutes to consider the importance of these small metal disks and how they contribute to holding our communities together. In addition, maybe you will also consider the demanding physical and technological requirements of the teams of surveyors who constructed the bench marks and performed the observations for the past 89 years.

Dave Doyle
Chief Geodetic Surveyor
National Geodetic Survey

PREFACE

In 1984, my parents took me on my first trip to Yellowstone National Park. I fell in love with the place and made a promise to myself that I'd bring my future wife here so that she, too, could see Mother Nature in all her glory. Six years later I got just that chance, and my new bride was just as enamored with Yellowstone as I had been. It has become a place of spiritual rebirth for us and since then, with the exception of the four summers we spent touring the country with a drum and bugle corps, we've made at least one pilgrimage per year to the park.

Yellowstone is an incredible place to be sure. There have been many superlatives used to describe the park and all of the wonders found there, including "Wonderland," first used by the *New York Times* in 1871. Former Chief Ranger Dan Sholly, in his 1991 book, *Guardians of Yellowstone*, referred to the park as "America's Cathedral to Mother Nature." The ever-changing features of the park are one thing that keeps us coming back year after year, and we've had numerous discussions about retiring to the area someday.

In late 2010, I quit a very nice job to begin working on a book related to Yellowstone's history. This required me to spend a summer in the park doing research for it and a couple of other projects I had going on. As a result, I needed to find a job in or near the park to allow me to support myself while I was there. I had the good fortune to land a job in the Yellowstone Association bookstore (YA) at the Old Faithful Visitor Education Center. It was my great pleasure to spend an entire summer meeting people from all over the planet who'd come to the world's first national park to explore its thermal features, wildlife, history, and its geology. I lost count of the number of times people were moved to tears relating how this spectacular place had touched them in the same manner it had my wife and me.

In addition to books and other educational materials, the YA stores sell collectible geodetic benchmark paperweights and lapel pins. They were fairly popular and quite often someone buying one of these would ask about the location of "real" benchmarks in the park, especially "...the one for Old Faithful." There were no lists available to provide to the customers, so I would often provide information about the small handful with which I was personally familiar. About midway through the summer it finally dawned on me that it'd be a good idea to produce a list of markers we could provide to customers when they asked these kinds of questions.

Having worked with the park's Spatial Analysis Center on previous projects, I contacted them about obtaining a list of the benchmarks; I figured maybe there were 100 or so, and it'd take me a few minutes to throw together a short list. When the data arrived, I was shocked to find well over 700 markers listed in locations all over the park's 2.2 million acres. I knew there'd be no way to produce a list of these that would be easy to distribute, so I began hunting for the "easy to find" markers in the immediate Old Faithful area. It became quite addictive, and in discussions with visitors, interpretive rangers, and others, there seemed to be a great deal of interest in having a master list or a book to guide people hunting for these markers as they moved about the park. Thus, the idea for *Benchmark Hunting in Yellowstone* was born.

ACKNOWLEDGMENTS

There are a variety of people to whom I owe a measure of gratitude in the preparation of this book.

First off, I need to thank the summer crew of the Yellowstone Association's South District I had the awesome privilege of working at the brand new Old Faithful Visitor Education Center during its first full summer of operation, getting to watch Old Faithful erupt hundreds of times. South District Manager Cherie Bardsley hired me, and I spent the summer working with her husband Cliff as my partner. The rest of the crew included Assistant Manager Bill Whetstone, and sales associates Jim and Pat Dick, Chuck and Nancy Siebert, Rich and Lynn Lane, Jeff and Pat Hansen, Gary and Jean Bowrey, and stockers Austin Barkdull, Cindy Henry, and Dee Holbrook (whose husband is the longest serving ranger in Yellowstone, with over 45 years of service in the park). Richard and Janet Nordlund, Ron and Marsha Hunzinger, and Ralph Mergen worked at the store in the Grant Village Visitor Center and the little information center at West Thumb, and Kathy Russell and Fred Jacobs had the great fortune of working at the scenic Madison Information Station at the foot of National Park Mountain. It was an absolute blast working and exploring the park with you guys, and I appreciate the encouragement you gave me to write this book.

The park's Spatial Analysis Center provided the data that formed the basis for the lists in this book. This was just the latest in a series of projects they've helped me with over the past couple of years. I am grateful for the work and guidance of Ann Rodman, the Center's Director, Senior GIS Technician Carrie Guiles, and most especially GIS technician Julie Rose, who has worked with me hand-in-hand on many different projects. You ladies have literally saved me untold numbers of hours, and I am forever in your debt. I know it's "part of [your] job," but you do it without complaining about my incessant requests for information, and this book simply would not have been possible without your help. Thank you.

Interpretive Ranger Kirrin Peart spent some time hunting for benchmarks (and a few other hidden oddities) with me in the Canyon area, including along the Otter Creek Service Road and old bear-feeding area the day after it was discovered that a grizzly bear had killed a hiker near Mary Mountain (before rangers closed the area). We spent a lot of time looking over our shoulders that day, and I was grateful for the company.

I'd also like to acknowledge the random customers who came through the Old Faithful and Albright Visitor Centers and stopped to discuss the subject of benchmarks, at great length in many cases. Those discussions were the impetus for this book. This includes Dr. Neil Weston, director of the National Spatial Reference System, the division of the National Geodetic Survey responsible for placing benchmarks these days. He brought his scout troop to Yellowstone and took them up to the summit of Mount Washburn to find the three markers there, and stopped by the store to purchase some souvenir benchmarks. Fate brought him to my register where we had quite a lengthy conversation about benchmarks in the park. He graciously offered to have the NGS install a new benchmark at Old Faithful, and I forwarded that offer to the park headquarters in Mammoth.

During the course of research for the book, I contacted several agencies inquiring about the history behind many of the benchmarks I found. To a person, everyone I spoke with was very gracious and related what information they could about the markers installed by their respective agencies or their predecessors. This included Wade Johnson of the Federal Highway Administration, Nancy Ward, the Chief of Maintenance for Yellowstone, Dan Dzurisin of the U.S. Geological Survey, and Dave Doyle, the Chief Geodetic Surveyor for the National Geodetic Survey. Thank you all for your time and willingness to do a little research and provide me with the information I requested.

And finally, I owe my lovely bride of 23+ years my undying gratitude for being willing to do without me for the six months I spent in Yellowstone. Her initial reaction to my asking her if I could spend the summer in the park was a mixture of anxiety at having to hold the fort down by herself for the half a year I was gone, and jealousy at not being able to go with me. I suppose I should thank the creators of Skype as well, for it was their software that allowed us to see each other every few days and thus keeping us connected. And despite the tremendous amount of fun I had, it just wasn't the same without you by my side. Thank you for allowing me the freedom to pursue my passion.

Table of Contents

PART IV: APPENDICES

INDEX OF PIDs

Part I: Background and History

Introduction

Yellowstone National Park was created as the world's first national park – the first space set aside from private development by a government for the specific purpose of allowing all of the people to enjoy that which Mother Nature has created (and continues to shape). Indeed, that purpose was specifically articulated in the park's organic legislation, signed by President Ulysses S. Grant on March 1, 1872: *For the Benefit and Enjoyment of the People.* The definition of what is seen as a national park has changed somewhat since that time, of course, but the idea behind the reasons for preserving the area "near the headwaters of the Yellowstone River"[1] remains the same.

Over three million people visit the area annually, each with their own favorite spaces or favorite things to do in or around the park. For some it's the wildlife; for others the mountains; for still others perhaps it's the rivers, lakes, and streams, or the cascades and spectacular waterfalls that lie along those ribbons of water. Some people are drawn to the park's geology – the vast mechanical processes that shape the park and have created its mountains and valleys and crafted the planet's largest collection of thermal features, including the world-renowned Old Faithful Geyser. And still others are infatuated with the history of the park – the vast body of information and knowledge about why Yellowstone is what it is, what man and nature have done here, and how all things have worked together to shape the area within and around the land dubbed "Wonderland" by early explorers and writers.

There are a wide variety of things to do and places to explore throughout the park's 2.2 million square acres. And though the vast majority of visitors only see the developed areas and perhaps some of the major outlying thermal features, there are some who like to get off the beaten path and see what else they can find. Doing this allows a person to explore facets of the park few people see on a regular basis, and often allows people to tie different aspects of the park together. Such is the case for those who seek out or hunt for survey markers.

Benchmark hunters, as they are known, are geocachers who enjoy searching for geodetic or engineering survey markers. In Yellowstone, these markers represent a unique nexus of the park's geology and its history, and with several hundred of them believed to exist throughout the vast expanse of Yellowstone, the opportunities for such exploration are rather robust. To aid in understand-

---

1 Quotes taken from the Yellowstone Park Act, Senate Bill S.392, signed into law on March 1, 1872.

ing where these markers can be found, why they're located where they are, and how to go about searching for them safely, this book has been created. So let's get started.

Geocaching and Benchmark Hunting

Geocaching is the game or sport of using GPS and Internet technologies to search for and find "geocaches," or collections of various items that people hide away specifically for the purpose of allowing or encouraging others to try to locate them. After someone hides a cache, they post a notice about it on a web site such as Geocaching.com.[2] Those who wish to search for a geocache can go to the website and enter search parameters (e.g., ZIP Code, city name, geocoordinates, etc.), retrieve a list of caches to search for along with their latitude and longitude and a description of how to find them, and then go out and try to locate the caches. When they've found one, the cache hunter might make an entry on an accompanying log book, exchange items in the cache for something they want to add to the cache, and then document or log their find on the Geocaching.com web site.

A geocache can take just about any form. Most are squirreled away in old ammunition boxes or plastic storage containers. Each geocache is carefully hidden so it takes some effort to find it. That's the fun part of geocaching – the thrill of the search and finding something tucked away; something unseen by the average person who happens to be passing by.

Geocaching in National Parks

The placement of geocaches as it is commonly practiced is illegal in national parks, however, including Yellowstone. There are several reasons for this:

- Cachers risk damaging the natural features of the park when they attempt to hide a geocache. Interfering with or damaging a park's features is prohibited.
- Over time, geocache hunters will often develop what are known as "social trails" leading to/from the caches they're hunting. This can negatively impact the park's natural or cultural features as well.
- Yellowstone is a geothermally active area, and persons attempting to hide a cache may wander into areas that are dangerous.
- Abandoning or establishing anything inside the park's boundaries without a permit is illegal, even if there is a specific purpose for it.

---

2 Though there are several different web sites related to the sport of geocaching, the Geocaching.com site is by far the largest and most popular.

For this reason, most people elect to search for "virtual" caches, Earthcaches[3], waypoints, or benchmarks within the parks, all of which are legal and even encouraged within Yellowstone. Questions concerning specifics regarding geocaching in the park should be addressed to the park's Visitor Services Office at 307-344-2107, or via e-mail at yell_visitor_services@nps.gov.

Benchmark Hunting

Benchmark hunting, or benchmarking, is the activity of searching for, locating, and documenting the find of geodetic survey markers, or benchmarks. It is similar to geocaching in that you're hunting for something unique most people aren't even aware exists, or that they ignore when they encounter. Unlike geocaching, however, the target of your hunt is something placed by government agencies for a specific purpose and not a random collection of materials.

With over 500 intact benchmarks in Yellowstone National Park, the potential for finding a significant number of markers is great. Searching for the markers has the added advantage of allowing you to simultaneously explore Yellowstone's vast wonderland. Many people find it quite invigorating to hunt for, locate, and document something that, in many cases, hasn't been seen in quite a few years.

Benchmarks

Benchmarks, or survey markers, are usually aluminum or brass discs about 3.5 inches in diameter. A typical disk is often inset into the top of a concrete pillar several feet tall which is buried vertically in the ground, its surface flush with its mount (or projecting slightly). Disks can also be set in bedrock, rock ledges, or in large boulders, and are sometimes set directly in the concrete of a large structure such as a bridge abutment, culvert headwall, the base of a high-tension electric tower, a road, or a sidewalk. Some are metal posts buried in the ground and covered by what are known as "Logo" caps. There are many other forms as well. One of the more unique markers within Yellowstone is an 18" x 24" block of granite with a survey rod embedded in the top of it. The mark's attributes are engraved on the sides of the block.

There are several purposes for benchmarks. They're placed primarily to document and establish a specific, known point (called a "control point") for the purpose of surveying, mapmaking, geologic monitoring, or some other technical purpose.[4] Some have been placed by volcano and earthquake monitoring

---

3 An Earthcache is a unique type of virtual cache designed to help people learn about a specific aspect of geoscience, and must be approved by NPS. There are approximately two dozen Earthcaches in Yellowstone as of this writing. See www.earthcache.org for details.
4 There are over a dozen different types of markers, each with its own purpose. For a detailed explanation of what they are and what each is used for, see the National Geodetic Survey's website at http://www.ngs.noaa.gov.

organizations specifically to keep track of the ground movements in and around the park. Most were placed prior to the widespread availability of technology and systems that allow for automated measurement of these changes today. In fact, because of the increasing accuracy of GPS and Interferometric Synthetic Aperture Radar (InSAR) technology, the placement of survey markers as a tool for surveying and mapmaking is on the wane, perhaps soon to be relegated to the dust bin of history. Established markers will remain in place so long as they are viable for reference purposes, however.

Benchmarks have been placed throughout the park by several different entities over the years, for a variety of purposes. The National Geodetic Survey (NGS) places markers to maintain a reliable geodetic control network for the nation[5]; the U.S. Geological Survey (USGS) installs markers to monitor ground deformation from seismic and volcanic activity throughout the park; and the Federal Highway Administration (FHWA) uses markers for road engineering purposes. With all of these overlapping surveys, it's not uncommon at all to find benchmarks from two organizations right next to each other.

Many of the markers throughout the park today were placed by the predecessors of organizations that exist today. For example, a substantial number of the benchmarks within the park date to 1923 when the Bureau of Public Roads (BPR) and the U.S. Coast and Geodetic Survey (USCGS) conducted the first large-scale elevation surveys of the park's road system. The BPR was the forerunner of today's FHWA, and from 1905 until 1939 was located in the U. S. Department of Agriculture (USDA). A handful of the markers were monumented (installed) by BPR during the years immediately after its name was changed from the "Office of Public Roads" in 1915; they even bear the additional imprint of the USDA (e.g., PY0806). And of course the USCGS was the forerunner of today's National Geodetic Survey, the organization that first comes to mind for most people when they think of survey markers.[6]

Benchmarks marked with the word "RESET" are those that were replaced due to the destruction of a previous marker. These typically retain the stamped characters from the previous marker plus the word "RESET." An example of this can be found on the Madison River Bridge on the West Entrance Road, known colloquially as "Seven Mile Bridge." In 1923, the BPR installed a benchmark on the bridge that existed at the time. In 1957, the original bridge was replaced with a newer, more modern structure (the bridge you see today). When the old bridge was destroyed the existing marker went with it, and a replacement marker was installed on the new structure bearing the same characters as the original (A14), plus the word "RESET" (PY0080).

---

5 A geodetic control network is the framework upon which other mapping and engineering surveys are conducted.

6 Geodesy is the branch of mathematical science that deals with the measurement of the earth.

Figure 1

Types of Benchmarks

Though there are several different kinds of benchmarks in use throughout the world, those in Yellowstone are primarily one of three types. The vast majority are the ubiquitous 3.5" brass or aluminum disks[7] embedded in concrete, rock, or the foundation of some structure such as a bridge or the headwall of a culvert (See Figure 1). Several of those installed in 1923 are located atop concrete pedestals protruding from the ground to a height of one to two feet (e.g., the one in front of the Albright Visitor Center). Many of those installed since the mid-1950s have been centered atop a long steel rod driven deep into the ground and protected by a five or six inch PVC pipe buried around it. When most people envision a benchmark, they almost invariably think of these. The center or highest point of the disk is the point from which measurements are taken.

Many of the newer markers installed by the NGS are 9/16" steel rods buried in the ground and covered by a 5" hinged cover known as a "Logo Cap" (See Figure 2). These are referred to as "3-D markers," and first saw use in the early 1980s. The stainless steel rod is driven into the ground as deep as it will go, and a small divot is made into the rounded top of the rod (the base of the leveling rod used by the surveyors slides down directly onto this pin). This is

Figure 2

the point from which measurements are taken. This style of marker is much more stable than most other types of installations, and is considered to be less susceptible to damage and disturbance due to surface activity. The primary disadvantage of these is that they are installed flush with the ground and can easily become covered by dirt, debris, and tree fall, making them very hard to locate. In many cases a metal detector is required to find them.

A third type of marker is the "pin" type often installed by the Federal Highway Administration. These are basically the same steel rods as those used by the NGS in their "Logo Cap" markers, but without the protection of the cap. These appear at or above ground level and are usually embedded in concrete (such as the one located on the concrete pad of the vault toilet at the Tuff Cliff Picnic Area) or rock. These rods also have a small divot on the top of

---

7 For a short time during World War II and immediately thereafter, cast iron was used for many benchmarks due to shortages of brass and bronze. Iron was also used in early NPS surveying.

them from which measurements are taken. The designator is often stamped or engraved on the side of the exposed portion of the pin. And along the old Mary Mountain Road/Trail between the Nez Perce Creek on the west side and Hayden Valley on the east side there are a number of markers that exist as spikes or designators chiseled directly into boulders.

Aside from those five types, the only examples of any other kind of marker include the granite block of the Lake Astro Station located in front of the Lake Lodge (discusssed below), and the Continuously Operating Reference Station (CORS)[8] located atop the seismic monitoring station near the old Mammoth school. This does not include the array of automated devices that can be found throughout the park, many of which also serve as GPS reference points. Data from all of these devices are available via the website of the Yellowstone Volcano Observatory (http://www.volcanoes.usgs.gov/yvo).

The vast majority of benchmarks set in Yellowstone are vertical controls – markers used to determine elevation above mean sea level. Far fewer are horizontal controls, those whose latitude and longitude are precisely known and serve as GPS reference points. As a general rule, markers with names stamped on them are horizontal controls (e.g., WASHBURN, YELLOWSTONE, KAYGEE, SHOSHONE, etc.), while those with a random series of numbers and/or letters are vertical controls (e.g., 21 MDC 1976, OF 5, 7766.345, etc.).

History of Benchmarks in Yellowstone

Today, there are several hundred benchmarks throughout the park, many of which date back almost a hundred years. The oldest one was installed 119 years ago and is still intact. Because of the unique geologic nature of the Yellowstone area, and the number of studies that have been conducted to determine what makes the place tick, the park has one of the highest densities of benchmarks in the country, if not the world. Several places exist where there are more than a dozen along a single linear kilometer. This makes the area a target-rich environment for the benchmark hunter.

Though there have been periodic installations or replacements of individual markers, the overwhelming majority of benchmarks were installed during one of the ten major surveys of the park. Understanding when and why these took place helps you understand why you find markers in specific places, why they're named a certain way, and why other markers are often found immediately adjacent to older ones.

---

8 CORS stations are electronic reference stations that continually update their three-dimensional positions for use by surveyors, meterologists, and others needing precise GPS measurements.

Early Surveys

In 1807, many years before Yellowstone existed as a national park, Congress created the U. S. Coast Survey. The primary function of this organization was to survey the new country's coastal areas in an attempt to set national boundaries, establish safe navigation pathways, and for other scientific purposes. At that time, inland surveys of public lands (which included the vast majority of western lands at this point) were conducted under the guise of an individual state or territory Surveyor General working for the General Land Office (GLO), a division of the U.S. Department of Interior. The GLO had been created in 1812 to oversee the surveying, managing, and selling of all public lands in the western United States. Since Congress could not at this time raise money through levying taxes on the country's citizens, it used the sale of public lands in the west as one of its primary means of funding government operations. General Henry D. Washburn had been named Surveyor General of the Montana Territory in 1869, and it was in this role that he organized the Washburn-Langford-Doane Expedition into the Yellowstone area in 1870.

In 1871, the Coast Survey was officially authorized to begin inland surveys as well, and in 1878, was renamed the U.S. Coast and Geodetic Survey (USCGS). The USCGS operated under its new name until 1970, when the agency was transferred to the U.S. Department of Commerce under the National Oceanic and Atmospheric Administration and renamed the National Geodetic Survey (NGS), the name it retains to this day.

The legislative act that renamed the USCGS also established the U.S. Geological Survey (USGS), consolidating geological and natural resource surveying into a single entity. Up to this point, such surveys had been undertaken by different groups, including the U.S. Army Corps of Engineers and individual state geological surveys. The USGS still exists by its original name today, and though it has many functions, most people know of it via its work related to earthquakes and volcanoes, fittingly cogent with respect to Yellowstone. The GLO remained largely intact through all of this and subsequent governmental reconstruction, and would go on to become what we know today as the Bureau of Land Management.[9] All of these organizations continue to conduct surveys as a part of their general responsibilities.

As a part of these surveys, engineers often install monuments or "benchmarks." These markers represent horizontal (latitude & longitude) and vertical (elevation) reference points that are used for conducting engineering studies, mapmaking, establishing boundaries, monitoring ground movement, and so

---

9 There are a small number of benchmarks in the Yellowstone backcountry that were installed in the early 1930s by the U.S. GLO. These were laid as a part of the surveys related to modifications to the park's northwestern boundaries during that time period. These markers are not included in this book, however.

forth. Early markers included everything from glass bottles and jars to buried seashells to simple marks chiseled into a static piece of concrete. Around the turn of the 20th century, the ubiquitous brass markers came into favor and remained the primary means of identifying survey points until the 1980s (and are still used today in many instances). Even today this is typically the first image that pops into a person's mind when they think of survey benchmarks.

The First Benchmark is Laid in Yellowstone

Many of the markers being installed by the new USCGS in the late 19th century were placed based on astronomical readings. These were known as "Astro" stations and were usually granite blocks; many of those installed during this era remain in place to this day. One of these was the Lake Astro Station, which remains intact near where it was originally installed in 1893 in front of the present day Lake Lodge.

At this point, perhaps a little context is in order. When the park was originally created, it was run by civilians under the direction of the U. S. Department of the Interior. There were few budgetary appropriations for the operation of the park, however, and the park began to suffer – wildlife was being poached, people stole artifacts and pieces of the thermal features, and there was little money available for the building or maintenance of roads and other structures necessary to facilitate tourist visitation. In 1886, using authority granted by Congress in 1883, the Department requested the U.S. Army take control of park operations to help stem the tide of damage and destruction of the park.

As a part of the military's management of the park, the U.S. Army Corps of Engineers assumed control of all road design and construction operations. In August of 1883, Engineer Lt. Dan Kingman arrived in Yellowstone and immediately set about laying out the road system.[10] He is widely credited with designing what eventually became known as the Grand Loop Road, the "Figure 8" road visitors still use to move about the park some 130 years hence. Over the subsequent five years, other engineers would continue Kingman's work and collectively began the process of building the road system he'd designed.

The Corps placed the first, albeit temporary survey markers in the park when they began constructing this new road system. These were generally itinerant markers used to lay out the road paths and were removed or plowed over as construction was completed. There's no known evidence of any of these markers anywhere in the park today.

---

10 The 1883 act that authorized the military to assist in the management and protection of the park immediately placed the Corps of Engineers in charge of road building and maintenance. Thus, Lt. Kingman and his engineering staff arrived that summer and set forth designing and building the park's road system.

In 1891, Engineer (then) Lt. Hiram M. Chittenden arrived in Yellowstone and assumed responsibility for completing the road system designed by Kingman. Much of the road network had been laid out in the western portions of the park by this time, but its eastern side was largely devoid of usable roadways. In order to properly complete his work, he needed a reference point from which to lay out his network of roads, preferably one located near the center of the park. He requested the U.S. Coast and Geodetic Survey (USCGS) establish such a point near Yellowstone Lake. Given that the park at this time was still in its original square shape, and the fact that this area was already somewhat developed (there was a store, a boat operation, and the Lake Hotel had just been completed), it represented a relatively centralized and easily accessible point from which he could begin his work.

The USCGS tasked a Mr. C. H. Sinclair with the job of laying out a survey line from Helena, Montana, to the point Chittenden had selected, and establishing its latitude and longitude. Sinclair arrived in Mammoth Hot Springs on May 30, 1892, but found the road to the lake area still blocked by significant snowpack. When Army soldiers finally cleared the snow, it still took him three days to travel the 52 miles due to the poor road conditions; it would be another week before he could get his instruments in place.

Sinclair managed to get the station ready to begin work on June 11th, but a broken telegraph circuit kept him from beginning his computations until June 23rd. Over the course of five nights, Sinclair made over 80 different calculations for latitude on 35 pairs of stars. When his aide, a Mr. G. R. Putnam, finally reached Helena and telegraph service had been restored, the pair was able to complete the longitudinal calculations over a period of another five days, finishing up on July 24. Temporary markers were laid at the end of the line until a stone monument could be carved in St. Paul, Minnesota, and delivered to the park in mid-1893.

Chittenden replaced the temporary marker with the new stone block (pictured), and it remains intact to this day.[11] Chittenden even makes reference to this marker in his 1895 book on the history of the park, *The Yellowstone National Park: Historical and Descriptive* (See the text box on the next page).

---

11 The original identifier (PID) for the marker was PY0011, but, according to common storytelling, the marker was hit by a car at some point and park surveyors "relocated" it to its current location (unknown why it wasn't put back in its original location). The reset of the monument is now PID PY0949. (The term "PID" is explained in Part II)

In 1895, Hiram M. Chittenden, then a Captain with the U.S. Army Corps of Engineers, wrote the first edition of his book, *The Yellowstone National Park: Historical and Descriptive*. Capt. Chittenden, who'd inherited the responsibility for carrying on the engineering of Yellowstone's road system from Lt. Dan Kingman, wrote eloquently about the park's history and geology as it was understood at the time. He also went to great lengths to explain each road segment (he was an engineer, after all) and highlight specific features the tourist should notice as s/he traveled through the park.

Hiram M. Chittenden

Chittenden begins his tour of the Lake area on page 248, "Just after the tourist leaves the Lake Hotel, he will see on the right of the roadway a small monument. It was placed there, in 1893, by the United States Corps of Engineers to mark a position accurately determined from astronomical observations by the United States Coast and Geodetic Survey in 1892. It is of value as a point of reference in surveys and other similar work." He provides its location as N44 33 16.1 W110 23 43.1 (the coordinates are carved into the stone), which would place it right in front of the existing Lake Lodge, approximately 187 feet southwest of where the granite marker actually rests today.

Chittenden would be responsible for finding the first route from Old Faithful to West Thumb via Craig Pass, and would design the road from the Grand Canyon to Tower Falls (though the engineer he left in charge didn't build it where he wanted it, but that's another story). Chittenden Road and Chittenden Bridge are both named in his honor. (*Image courtesy National Park Service*)

In 1899, a team from the nascent U.S. Geological Survey conducted a series of triangulation surveys through Yellowstone and into the Jackson Valley south of the park. They "discovered" that the latitude and longitude measurements provided by the USCGS were inaccurate, attributing this to "station error," because of "...the great mass of mountains south and west of [Mount] Sheridan." In reality, however, the USGS measurements were wildly inaccurate, providing locations several hundred feet from where the marker actually lay (the coordinates USCGS originally provided were reasonably accurate for the day). There's no evidence the granite marker was ever moved as a result of this new finding, however. Had they done so, it would have ended up in the large field between the Lodge and Topping Point (the cluster of trees on the edge of the lake looking east from the porch of the lodge).

From this point until the time automobiles were allowed into the park in 1915, there were no (known) further surveys conducted. The "roads" for the stagecoaches were simply dirt or gravel roads and were built according to U.S. Army engineering protocols. Within a year, though, it became obvious that automobiles and the horses drawing stagecoaches weren't going to be able to coexist on the narrow roads built during this period. The decision to ban stagecoaches was made, and over the course of the next several years the road system would gradually be reworked to serve the automobile.

For an eight-year period of time, shortly after the National Park Service was created, from 1918 until 1926, the NPS itself managed its own road construction projects, though relatively little actual construction occurred due to lack of funding. Some construction planning did take place, especially along the North Entrance Road. A handful of markers installed during this period bear "USDI" and "NPS" stampings and are made of cast iron. They are quite rare in the park. The only known remaining marker (of approximately 20) is located just north of the Mammoth Campground (PY0158).

The First Large-Scale Surveys are Conducted in Yellowstone

In 1923, the U. S. Coast and Geodetic Survey (USCGS) and the Bureau of Public Roads (BPR) independently undertook the first full-scale leveling surveys (elevation determination) of Yellowstone. For the USCGS the work in Yellowstone was merely an extension of the land surveys they'd begun in 1878. The BPR had a different reason for conducting their surveys, however.

As one of the first major federal highway projects in the country, there had already been some discussion of the BPR assuming responsibility for the construction of roads within Yellowstone. Though initially hesitant to embrace turning over building of park roads to an "outside" agency, Superintendent Horace Albright eventually came to believe that BPR and its staff of engineers who specialized in highway construction might be better suited to manage such projects in conjunction with landscape architects from the National Park Service. A number of meetings and conversations was had between NPS, BPR, and senior officials in the Department of Interior in Washington, DC, before the final decision was made.

In 1926, management of road projects was formally turned over to the Bureau of Public Roads through a cooperative agreement between the agencies (a relationship that continues to this day with BPR's successor, the Federal Highway Administration). BPR would design and let contracts for the construction of the roads while the NPS would be responsible for designing the landscape, guardrails and other "design" features of the roads built under BPR's auspices. As a prelude to that agreement, the BPR undertook their 1923 survey of the road system throughout the park to determine the precise elevations along the existing roads.

These surveys were undertaken from late July to early November, and covered the entire road system that existed within the park up to that point, with the exception of the Northeast Entrance Road (which was about to undergo major reconstruction, and the exact path of the new road had not been determined with any finality). Therefore, as you search for markers today, you'll see 1923-era benchmarks from both the USCGS and BPR throughout the park, oftentimes immediately adjacent to markers installed during subsequent surveys.

Approximately half the markers installed during this era are not included in this edition of the book because of the necessity of hiking into the backcountry to reach them. Many of these were installed along what in 1923 were the park's primary thoroughfares, but are now bypassed and used for trails or have been completely abandoned. These include:

- The old Turbid Lake road segment between what is today the Pelican Creek Trailhead and the nearly hairpin curve on the East Entrance Road approximately 8/10th of a mile east of Lake Butte Drive.
- The old segment of the road between the Natural Bridge Trailhead and Arnica Creek along the road between West Thumb and Lake Village (which is today part of the largely abandoned Howard Eaton Trail).
- The old segment of road that used to run through Norris Geyser Basin between the north end of Elk Park and its original intersection near the present day campground.
- The old stage road between Fountain Flats and Hayden Valley (the western half of which is part of what is today the Mary Mountain Trail). This road paralleled the Nez Perce Creek to Mary Lake, and then proceeded northeast to Highland Hot Springs before swinging south and paralleling Dry Creek and Trout Creek to today's road through Hayden Valley.
- The northern segment of the old South Entrance Road from what is today the junction at Grant Village to just north of Lewis Lake (at the present day Lewis Lake/Dogshead Trailhead)
- The southern segment of the old South Entrance Road from two miles south of Lewis Falls to two miles north of the existing South Entrance Station.
- The old segment of road between DeLacy Creek (east of Craig Pass) and West Thumb Junction.
- The old segment of road between the Gibbon Falls overlook and Tanker's Curve. Interestingly, the newly constructed road through this area is the route of the original road through this area, even though it doesn't have any benchmarks along it.

A GPX file with the PIDs and approximate latitude and longitude coordinates for all of the markers in these segments is available at this book's website. See Appendix 3 for information on how to obtain and use the file.

In some areas, road construction has destroyed many of the original 1923 markers. The road between Tower Junction and Canyon Junction has been rerouted and reconstructed several times, and none of the original 1923 markers remain except for one in the Tower Campground and the one on Chittenden Road at the parking area for the summit trailhead. The marker near Tower Junction is adjacent to where the original road terminates just east of one of the campsites. Along the road between Madison Junction and Norris Junction, the only original marker that remains is the one installed at the Gibbon Falls Overlook.

In 1929 and through the early 1930s, a series of surveys were done as a result of legislation authorizing the additions to Yellowstone and alterations to its boundaries. These studies were done by the General Land Office (today's Bureau of Land Management). There are a handful of markers and boundary stakes along the park's old and new boundaries, especially in the northwestern section of the park inside Montana. One example is the T2856M marker installed in 1931 by the GLO along the trail to High Lake.[12]

In 1936, 1941, and 1955, leveling surveys were completed by the U.S. Geological Survey (USGS) to verify and update measurements obtained during the initial USCGS surveys completed in 1923. The 1936 surveys concentrated on a section of the park along the Northeast Entrance Road from Tower Junction to the Slough Creek Campground Road, and surveys in 1941 focused on the Northeast Entrance Road from Slough Creek to the Northeast Entrance Station.[13] The Northeast Entrance Road had been the subject of great debate for almost a decade prior to its completion, and thus hadn't been surveyed during the Geodetic Survey's original foray through the park in 1923.

It was during this period the Bureau of Public Roads underwent several changes. In 1939, President Roosevelt continued a sweeping reorganization of federal agencies begun earlier in the Great Depression. Among his creations was the Federal Works Agency[14], into which the BPR was subsumed, becoming the Public Roads Administration (PRA). This new entity was responsible for undertaking the 1941 surveys of the Northeast Entrance Road in parallel with the work of the USGS (described above). The FWA was short-lived,

---

12 The marker is located at 45.05238, -110.93297, approximately ½ mile east of High Lake along the Specimen Creek Trail. None of these GLO markers appear in this book.
13 Construction of the western section of the Northeast Entrance Road had been completed by 1936, and much of the balance by 1941. This is the reason for the two different surveys.
14 The FWA also included the Works Progress Administration, the largest and perhaps most infamous of the "New Deal" agencies created by President Roosevelt.

however. In 1949, the agency was dissolved and the Bureau of Public Roads was reconstituted into the Department of Commerce, where it remained until 1966, when the Federal Highway Administration was created in the Department of Transportation (where it remains to this day). As a result the Northeast Entrance Road is one of the only stretches of roadway in the park along which you'll see benchmarks stamped with the PRA/FWA imprints. Following the 1941 work by PRA and the USGS, Yellowstone's entire road system, as it existed at that time, had been surveyed and marked at least once.

In 1950, the USCGS established a series of triangulation points throughout Yellowstone, including on many of the park's major peaks. Mt. Washburn, Mt. Sheridan, Mt. Holmes, Purple Mountain, and several other major points were surveyed and had benchmarks installed during the late summer. Today, the three markers installed at the summit of Mt. Washburn are some of the most popular markers in the park for benchmark hunters. A set of these benchmarks was also installed just east of the Lake Ranger Station (along the old roadbed, approximately 490+/- feet east of the station at ground level. See PY0948). Additional markers were installed on lesser peaks such as Pelican Cone, Observation Peak, and Bunsen Peak by the U.S. Geological Survey during this period as well (specifically 1955-1958).

The 1955 surveys occurred across the Central Plateau along the old stage road between the Fountain Flat area and Hayden Valley along what today is the Mary Mountain Trail and the old Trout Creek Stagecoach Road (which was still being used as a "fire road" at that point). Many of the elevation measurements taken during this period were "off" from those obtained during placement of markers in 1923. At the time, this was believed to be due to inaccuracies in the previous surveys.

Earthquakes, Volcanoes, and Benchmarks

Most of the significant benchmark installations in the latter half of the 20th Century came about because of earthquake activity in the park and surrounding areas, and the realization that Yellowstone sat atop an active volcano. In 1960, the USCGS did survey work along the stretch of road from the West Entrance to Madison Junction, Madison to Norris, and Norris to Mammoth Hot Springs, in response to the Hebgen Lake Earthquake that rocked the area in 1959. These surveys were designed specifically to study ground deformation along the western side of the park as a consequence of seismic activity. [15]

---

15 The Hebgen Lake Earthquake struck at 11:37PM local time on August 17, 1959, and was centered some 15 miles north of the town of West Yellowstone near Hebgen Lake on the Madison River. The 7.5 earthquake destroyed several buildings nears its epicenter and damaged several facilities (including the Old Faithful Inn) and roadways inside the park. No one was injured in the park, but several were killed near the quake's epicenter.

In the mid-1970s (1975-1977), subsequent to the Yellowstone Park earthquake[16], the USGS began installing additional benchmarks throughout the park. These markers, too, were placed specifically to measure ground deformation and were installed throughout the park's midsection. Surveys performed during the placement of these markers showed a rise of as much as 72cm from the elevations of markers installed in 1923, especially on the park's eastern side through Hayden Valley and around the northern shore of Yellowstone Lake. Geologists determined these variations were caused by actual uplift of the earth's crust. Later work would discover small errors in the 1975-77 surveys as well, but the net result was increased interest in the geophysics of the Yellowstone Caldera.

From 1983 to 1986, the USGS conducted another round of technical studies in Yellowstone under the auspices of the Volcanic Hazards Reduction Program. From 1983 through 1985, researchers installed several series of new markers along the Canyon Village to Lake Butte line specifically to monitor the rise and fall of the crust along the road between Canyon Village and the Lake and along the Lake's northern boundary to Lake Butte. This was the area that showed the most significant deformation in the 1970s studies relative to those undertaken in 1923. In October of 1983, these surveys showed additional rise since the 1976 study, and the September, 1984, revisitation of these same benchmarks showed still additional uplift from the year before. The follow-up 1985 surveys (also in September) showed no changes, but when the area was resurveyed during the September, 1986, visits, the same areas had subsided by as much as 25mm at some locations. Interestingly, the work on this project had begun shortly after October 1, 1983, and less than one month later, the park was rocked by the Borah Peak earthquake.[17]

The 1986 survey work also included a series of brand new markers along the roadway from Lewis Lake to West Thumb to Old Faithful to Madison Junction to study the western edge of the Yellowstone Caldera. These markers supplemented those originally installed in 1923, many of which had been resurveyed in 1976, but that were along now abandoned segments of roadway and thus no longer readily accessible to the survey teams. Patterns of lift similar to what had been seen in the Canyon to Lake Butte area relative to localized measurements taken in 1923 and 1976 were noted along this line as well.

---

16 This magnitude 6.1 earthquake was centered just south of the road between Norris Junction and Canyon Junction, approximately halfway between the two. It occurred at 12:45PM local time on June 30, 1975. No damages were recorded as a result of the temblor or any of its aftershocks.

17 The Borah Peak Earthquake struck at 8:06AM local time on October 28, 1983 near Borah Peak, WNW of Idaho Falls. The magnitude 7.3 quake was felt throughout the park, but only minor damages were reported. This included approximately 100 feet of the viewing platform at Inspiration Point dropping off into the Grand Canyon (no one was on it at the time, fortunately).

All of this work was undertaken by the U.S. Geological Survey's Cascades Volcano Observatory, which had been created in the aftermath of the 1980 Mt. Saint Helen's eruption. This is why you see the characters "CVO" stamped into markers installed during this period. At the time, the Yellowstone Volcano Observatory (YVO) didn't exist, so the CVO had been given the responsibility for surveying and monitoring the Yellowstone area until 2001, when the YVO was created at the University of Utah as a cooperative venture between the university, the USGS, and the National Park Service.

In 1987, the USGS contracted with the NGS to conduct a new leveling survey of the entire park and install a new series of markers to aid in further deformation studies. This represented the first full-scale, park-wide surveys since the original leveling surveys were undertaken in 1923. Benchmarks from all of these surveys remain in place and are revisited periodically as an adjunct to the measurements provided by the automated devices now used to monitor ground deformation throughout the park. This was to be the last major installation of benchmarks in Yellowstone.

In the late 1990s, the USGS began installing automated monitoring systems throughout Yellowstone to measure ground deformation. These devices send continuous updates about ground movement in the park and are considerably more accurate than the manual measurements taken at the survey markers. The YVO manages the program, and the general public can monitor the rise and fall of the ground in the park through their website.[18]

Interestingly, the studies conducted during the 1986-1995 time period showed subsidence in those areas that had risen between 1923 and 1986. Between 1983 and 2007 the ground rose and fell in many places throughout the park, in fact. The data collected from the vast array of benchmarks and automated monitoring devices installed at various locations throughout the park demonstrated that Yellowstone is "breathing" – the ground is literally rising and subsiding in several different locations throughout the park. This is one reason why these historical surveys, and the benchmarks installed as a part of those studies, have played such a pivotal role in understanding the area's complex geological processes.

Other Surveys

In 1977, the National Park Service began planning for upgrades to many of the park's water and wastewater systems. As a part of that, NPS engineers surveyed areas where water intakes, supply lines, and reservoirs might be placed. Other points of reference were surveyed during this period as well. These surveys resulted in approximately two dozen additional benchmarks being placed in

---

18 The YVO website can be found at http://www.volcanoes.usgs.gov/yvo

various locations throughout the park. Examples can be seen today around Mammoth, in front of the Lake Hotel, along the Otter Creek Service Road, in the Canyon area, near Mystic Falls (at the Upper Geyser Basin Overlook), and at the West Thumb Geyser Basin among other places. Sadly, many of these markers were not well documented, and many may have been lost.

In 1986, the Federal Highway Administration began a multi-year, multi-phase project to rebuild and rehabilitate the park's Grand Loop Road and the entrance roads. As a part of this process, they installed several dozen benchmarks throughout the park, and undertook an aerial photographic survey and several engineering studies. The photographs and studies were used to develop the *Parkwide Road Improvement Plan: Yellowstone National Park*, which was completed in June of 1992. The document was the foundation of a 20-year plan to rehabilitate and improve the road system and bring it up to current design standards. The photos and the survey markers have been used in the various road construction projects undertaken as a part of that plan (which has extended well beyond the plan's projected 20 year scope, due in large part to budgetary issues).

A few replacement markers have been installed since the late 1980s and the FHWA continues to install occasional markers when they're performing engineering studies for new road construction projects throughout the park. But with the advent of highly accurate GPS-based survey meters, and the automated ground deformation and seismic monitoring systems in place throughout the park today, few new markers are being installed.

One additional unique station that bears mentioning is the Continuously Operating Reference Station (CORS) located just east of the old elementary school in the Lower Mammoth Housing Area. This is an automated station owned by the Plate Boundary Observatory installed in 1998 to provide continuous, real-time GPS data to various research and governmental agencies. The station is co-located with a USGS seismic monitoring station located in a vault beneath the hill where the CORS station rests.

Where's the Benchmark for Old Faithful?

One of the most often searched for benchmarks in Yellowstone is the marker once located at Old Faithful. The original benchmark "E-10 1923" (PY0046) was listed as being located "50 yards southwest of the crater of Old Faithful Geyser, and at the center of a parking space,"[19] with an elevation of 7366.567 feet (at one time the "official" elevation of the Old Faithful area was listed as 7366 feet based on the reading ascertained during the placement of the

---

19 Quote taken from the NGS Datasheet for PY0046

Old Faithful benchmark, in fact). This original monument was installed on a concrete pedestal that rose 17" from the ground at the head end of the center parking space in front of the geyser. At the time, you could park your car right in front of the geyser and watch it erupt. As you might imagine, traffic flow through the area was somewhat less than optimal.

In 1964, the original E-10 monument was removed because it was in danger of being hit by automobiles, and a replacement monument was "reset" a few yards away, flush with the ground in the easternmost parking spot in front of Old Faithful. This new monument didn't last long, however. When the new (existing) road system around the Old Faithful area was completed and opened in 1972, most of the older roads through the area and the parking spaces in front of the geyser were reclaimed and restored to sand/gravel walkways. No one is sure what happened to the E-10 or E-10 RESET markers themselves. They may be buried under the sand, may have been hauled off to landfills, or someone may have absconded with either or both of them for their personal collections.

An untold number of hours has been spent surveying and installing the benchmarks around Yellowstone National Park. Almost every one of them remains a valuable tool in helping engineers and scientists do their work. Understanding the history behind them and why they have been placed where they are makes searching for them that much more intriguing. As you go about hunting for the markers, please keep this in mind and ensure that you do not do anything to damage the markers or make them unusable for those who might need them in the future.

Part II: Hunting for Benchmarks

Introduction

This book assumes the reader has a basic understanding of geocaching principles, knows basic GPS operation, has a working knowledge of compass use and navigation skills, and can use a tape measure or estimate short distances. If you lack an understanding of these principles, let me suggest you purchase a book geared specifically toward geocaching. "*Geocaching for Dummies*" is an excellent starting point. You might also consider "*GPS for Dummies*" as well if you are not familiar with the operation and limitations of the GPS system and receivers. Both are excellent introductions to their respective subject matter, and the information contained within them will be of invaluable assistance as you go about hunting for benchmarks in Yellowstone.

This book provides a list of approximately 300 benchmarks located within the boundaries of Yellowstone National Park. The listings are organized by road segment, since most people will look for these as they move through the park from one development to another. You can turn to the specific road segment, which explains where to set your odometer or GPS to zero, and then travel in the direction indicated, stopping where noted to find each marker.

The printed version of this book is designed to allow for easy transport into the field while you use it to hunt for benchmarks. It's best to have as much information available to you when you're trying to locate the markers, rather than relying simply on geographic coordinates. The "to reach" verbiage is often hard to memorize, so having the book at your disposal can be quite the time-saver. It is small enough to keep in a gallon-sized Ziplock bag to keep it from getting wet or dirty.

This book differs from the standard NGS data sheets in that A) the GPS coordinates are much more accurate (for the vertical markers) and have been verified, and B) the verbal locator ("To Reach") information has been reduced to a succinct version to allow the user to quickly decode the directions on how to find the markers.

As you find each marker, you can check it off and enter any notes you wish in the space provided. You might note the date, time, and conditions under which you found it, or any difficulties you had locating it. If the book's coordinates are off, you might also note the coordinates provided to you by your GPS device if you're using one. And, if you take photographs of your find, you might wish to notate which image numbers are of that particular marker for future reference.

Not Intended for Technical or Scientific Purposes

This book is written for those individuals interested in locating benchmarks as a hobby, and not for any scientific or technical purposes. It therefore provides a limited and simplified set of data for each marker. If you need information about the markers for technical work, you're encouraged to obtain the original data sheets from the National Geodetic Survey.

How to Use the Information in These Lists

Most people travel around the park in an organized fashion, moving from one development or attraction to another, and thus, one junction to another. The lists are therefore organized by road segment, beginning with the North Entrance Road and traveling clockwise around the Figure 8 road known as the Grand Loop Road. The other four entrance roads appear in the list where they intersect with the Grand Loop Road.

Each segment's markers are listed in order of distance from one of the park's main road junctions. Approximately half of the markers for each segment are listed from one junction and the other half from the opposite junction. This is done to allow the book's lists to remain consistent with the manner in which the NGS database describes the markers. It also allows the reader to compare the data sheets with the book in case the book contains an error or in the event the reader wishes to use additional information from the datasheets.

Drive the estimated distance looking for any landmarks that are referenced in the verbal description of how to find the marker. The vast majority of markers are located within relatively easy walking distance from a road pullout. Keep an eye on your odometer/GPS unit, and when you're at the mileage indicated, pull over to the side of the road (ensuring your vehicle is completely out of the traffic pattern). Exit your vehicle and try to locate the marker using the information provided in the "To Reach" notations.

If you're unable to find it using the verbal descriptions, attempt to locate it with your GPS unit. Again, you are encouraged to take the book with you on your search, since it is often not possible to remember all of the details for each marker. When you find the benchmark, confirm that the characters stamped into it agree with what's in that marker's entry. Photograph it, GPS it, and make any notes you feel appropriate. If you're moved to do so, log onto geocaching.com and document your find there as well.

GPS Use and Limitations

The GPS coordinates provided in the tables of this book were acquired using a Garmin 60CSx handheld receiver. The device is accurate to within three to five meters, though in some instances that accuracy may have been impacted by things such as tree cover. If you arrive at the coordinates provided and do not find the specified marker, broaden your search to a radius of as much as 25-30 feet from your location. Keep in mind most markers are at ground level and may be covered with dirt or debris, or a recently fallen tree.

Information Sources

The original data for this book was obtained from Yellowstone's Spatial Analysis Center, and was derived from the National Geodetic Survey (NGS) database, which is dated in the year 2000. Additional data were derived from material provided by the Yellowstone Volcano Observatory. The data were organized into road segments, and then each marker was located and visually inspected, its geolocation ascertained, and the stamping verified. Markers that were far off the beaten path, those that could not be found, and those whose stamping did not match the information from the database were removed from the list produced for this book. Benchmarks for which there was no safe pullout nearby, or for which traffic or personal safety issues might present a problem during the accessing of the markers have likewise not been included in this book. And, finally, many of the markers that are listed in the NGS database have been destroyed due to road construction throughout the park and of course are not to be found in these pages. For information about the limitations of the material in the NGS database, see the NGS website at http://www.ngs.noaa.gov.

During the search for benchmarks identified in the database, approximately two dozen undocumented markers were found. These include the marker at the Upper Geyser Basin Overlook near Mystic Falls and an old BPR marker located south of the Old Faithful Lodge, for example. Chances are good that there are additional markers lying around the park that have not been documented. For example, one of the markers at the Old Faithful Interchange bridge is stamped "OF-4", and the marker near Mystic Falls is stamped "OF-5." There is a reasonable likelihood that three additional markers (OF-1 through OF-3) exist around the Old Faithful area somewhere, but they have not been located as yet. If you come across a marker not identified herein, you are encouraged to let me know via e-mail or via the book's website (See Appendix 3).

Logging Your Finds

With a typical geocache find, you often enter a notation in a log book that you find with the cache itself. With benchmarks, there are web sites available for you to indicate that you've found each marker. The most popular of these is geocaching.com. You can create a free account there and enter both verbiage and photos for each find you make. As of this writing, only about one third of the park's benchmarks have been noted as "found" on Geocaching's website.

There are specific rules for reporting the different types of markers on the Geocaching site; see their website for details. Entering good notes into this book when you make a find will help you make better entries on such web sites, and may make it a bit easier for others who use your information in the future.

Reporting Errors & Changes

The information concerning the location of benchmarks contained within this list has been verified by the author or someone known to be authoritative by the author, and is believed to be accurate as of the date this book was published.

Over the course of time, however, markers are destroyed when new roads or bridges are built, when heavy machinery moves through areas, or when covered by dirt, debris, grass or fallen trees. Additionally, Yellowstone is a geologically active area, and is subject to ground motion that may displace the occasional marker (think rockslides, earthquakes, etc.). And, occasionally, errors are made in data entry. As a result, even those listed herein as confirmed may be tough to find when you go looking for them. If you do encounter one that has been destroyed, or is no longer accessible, please notify me via e-mail or via the book's website.

Similarly, if you come across a benchmark not found in this book, let me know. Send me the geographic coordinates (if you have a GPS device) and a description of where you found it relative to any local landmarks. If possible, please include a close-up photograph of the marker and a "context" photo that shows the marker in its surroundings. If a photograph isn't possible, please provide me with the characters that are stamped into the top of the marker. This will allow me to verify which marker it is. If it is one that I've not listed, I'll add it to the next edition.

If you encounter a marker that has been damaged, destroyed, or removed, you are encouraged to photograph and report it to the appropriate agency via the NGS web site at http://www.ngs.noaa.gov. You should never damage or remove any marker you find, as doing so is a violation of federal law and may result in a fine. For markers not found in the NGS database (including those listed herein with PIDs beginning with "PY99" or "QX99"), report damages to the park's Geology Division at 302-344-2441.

Safety in Yellowstone

Yellowstone can be a dangerous place for anyone who does not understand and respect the park and its thermal features, wildlife, and the other features that make it what it is. It is important that you observe certain safety precautions as you travel through the park attempting to locate these markers.

Thermal Features: Many of the benchmarks identified in this book are located near one or more of the park's thermal features. You are required by law to stay on boardwalks where they're provided, and to remain outside the boundaries of any closed areas. People have been severely burned when their feet have broken through the thin crust. Watch where you walk!

Road Safety: The vast majority of the benchmarks in this book are alongside or adjacent to the park's roads. When you stop to attempt to locate the markers, try to park in one of the numerous pullouts. If that's not possible, at a minimum ensure your vehicle is completely off the roadway (all four wheels) and will not interfere with traffic flow. When exiting your vehicle, be sure you look before you open your door and step out, especially if you're parked right off the side of the roadway. When re-entering the roadway, be sure and look in both directions before you pull out. Heed all signs regarding restricted or closed areas.

Climbing/Hiking: Many of the markers are located on top of rock formations, on cliff sides, and on other features that require you to hike or climb to reach them. Be sure you wear appropriate footwear and are equipped with hiking gear if you set out to find markers located in these areas. Some markers require an extensive hike to reach (i.e., those on the summits of mountains). Be sure you are familiar with the park's hiking regulations and are appropriately equipped (including bear spray!!!) for long distance hikes when searching for these. Inquire at the nearest backcountry office prior to attempting these finds.

Bear Management Areas/Wildlife Closures: Some of the benchmarks identified herein are located within bear management areas. These areas are closed intermittently, especially during the early part of the spring season as the bears begin coming out of hibernation. As with the thermal areas, you are required to remain outside areas closed for wildlife management purposes. Failure to do so may result in personal harm and/or a citation.

Wildlife Safety: Park regulations require you to remain 25 yards away from all wildlife, except for bears and wolves, for which the distance is 100 yards. Do not harass wildlife or try to get them to move so you can find a benchmark. Simply return to the location at a later time. If you approach wildlife close enough that they move away from you, you're too close. Getting too close to an animal may result in harm to you or perhaps even the loss of your life.

Weather: The weather is very changeable in Yellowstone. Dress appropriately (think layers!), monitor the weather forecasts, and plan accordingly, especially if you plan on hiking into the backcountry looking for these markers.

Backcountry Benchmark Hunting

While the vast majority of the benchmarks listed in this book are within a few hundred feet of the roadway, a small number are located several miles from the nearest road. Additionally, as I outlined earlier, a significant number of the older benchmarks are located along old, abandoned roadbeds. Hunting for the markers in these areas will require hiking through backcountry areas with all of the attendant dangers that entails.

Before you elect to head off into remote areas in search of benchmarks, you are highly encouraged to familiarize yourself with the rules, regulations, and guidelines for backcountry use in Yellowstone. The best place to start is the park's web site, which can be found at www.nps.gov/yell. It is a good idea to stop by one of the park's Backcountry Offices to check in and get any updates on conditions prior to heading out, especially as they relate to the latest bear activity. Note that overnight camping in the backcountry requires a permit, which can be obtained through one of the Backcountry Offices as well.

Leave No Trace

In order to minimize your impact on the park, its wildlife, its flora, and the natural environment, you should do everything possible to keep from damaging the park's natural features. "Leave No Trace" is a concept that states you should do as much as you can to prevent anyone from knowing you've even been in an area. You should take all of your trash out with you when you leave a campsite, for example. If you see the beginnings of a trail developing in an area, take a route that avoids this trail so that you don't contribute to it. If you hike with a group of people, ensure each one uses a different route to get to the same location where possible, and use different routes on your way out. Basically, you should do what you can to minimize your impact on an area, and leave it so that anyone who follows you cannot tell anyone has even been in the area.

Conventions

The lists in the following section are broken down into sixteen sections that correspond to individual road segments, plus one "miscellaneous" section for benchmarks that are not located along one of the major road segments. The breakouts assume you're traveling through the park in a clockwise fashion commencing from the park's North Entrance at the Roosevelt Arch.

Each entry provides you with the information needed to find the listed benchmark and verify what you've found is the correct one. The following naming and documentation conventions apply to the entries provided in the following tables:

PID: The PID is the "permanent identifier" of the bench mark. These are assigned by the National Geodetic Survey (NGS) as a way to track specific markers. The PID does not appear on the marker itself, but is used to locate the marker in the NGS database or on sites such as geocaching.com. If you use the waypoint feature on your GPS to store location data for the markers, the PID is a good identifier to use.

Those benchmarks that do not appear in the NGS database are identified within this book with PIDs beginning with "PY99" or "QX99." These numbers were assigned by the author specifically for the purpose of allowing them to be included in this book. These have not been assigned "official" PIDs by the NGS (there's a technical process that has to be followed for that to happen, and many of these markers have not gone through that for one reason or another[1]), and in order to provide a way of tracking them and including them in the tables, they needed to have their own PIDs. Note that you also cannot use these PIDs to locate the markers in Geocaching's database. The Geocaching website has a procedure to follow for adding markers that do not have PIDs. See their web site for details.

The first two letters of the PID are known as the "prefix" and indicate which map grid the benchmark exists in.[2] All benchmarks within the park south of the 45th parallel have PIDs that begin with "PY," while those markers north of the 45th parallel have PIDs beginning with "QX." The numbers themselves are purely random. There are at least four benchmarks that begin with the prefix "CQ." These are reference marks for one of the nearby azimuth markers (see the NGS web site for specifics on the purpose of these markers). The identifier for the CORS Station at Mammoth begins with "AI." There is a complete index of all of the PIDs that appear in these lists at the end of the book.

Stamp: The monument stamp is a series of characters stamped into the bench mark as a means of identifying the marker. There is no set format for these, and they're set by the organization placing the marker based on whatever criteria they are using at the time. This is the best way to determine whether or not you've found the exact marker referred to in each entry in the list. If the stamp is different than what you find in this book, there's a good chance you've found another marker, perhaps even one I've missed altogether. Recall that those with names are horizontal (GPS) control marks, while those with what appears to be random sequences of characters are typically vertical (elevation) control marks.

---

1 That process is known as "bluebooking," and is a methodology used to ensure the marker is placed according to standards set by the NGS. It costs several hundred dollars per marker to have this done, so some agencies don't bother to go through this process.

2 The NGS maintains a map that shows the PID prefixes. See the boo's website for a link to this map, along with other resources to aid you in your hunts.

Family: Benchmarks that are located in or near developments, features, and points of interest, and are easily accessible to families with smaller children are identified with a "Y." See Appendix B for a complete list of "family-friendly" benchmarks.

Access: Bench marks are listed as "accessible" (Y) if they can be reached safely by someone in a wheelchair. While many markers listed as inaccessible can be reached by a wheelchair, some of these would require the chair-bound person to move into or through the flow of traffic, resulting in a danger to both the benchmark hunter and traffic. Therefore, these are listed as inaccessible. Appendix A contains a list of specific markers determined to be accessible.

Ease: This is a subjective measure of the ease with which the casual searcher should be able to find the markers. Those located adjacent to roadways, on bridges or other structures accessible with minimal effort are listed as "E," for "easy." Those that are located far off the road, those that may be buried by dirt, debris, or that require some unique navigation to reach are listed as "M" for "moderate." Those that require a substantial off-road hike, climbs of hills or rocky ledges, or are in relatively inaccessible locations (including the backcountry) are listed as "D" for "difficult."

Coordinates: This is the latitude and longitude measured in decimal degrees. This information is derived from readings obtained when the marker was confirmed, using a handheld GPS device. Keep in mind that GPS is accurate only within a few feet of any given point, so if you don't see the marker at the specific coordinates given within this list, survey the area around you (typically within 10-30 feet or so).

Elevation: This is a measurement of elevation (expressed in feet above mean sea level) based on information provided by the NGS or the body that placed the marker. These figures have NOT been confirmed through independent observation, however. For many of the markers, the actual elevation may be slightly higher or lower than the elevation stamped on the benchmark. Recall that in the 1970s, it was discovered many of the benchmarks in the park had risen from the levels ascertained in the 1923 surveys due to ground uplift. What you see listed here is what is given in the NGS database (or from handheld GPS measurement for those not in the NGS database) and often represents an adjusted value in elevation due to uplift and subsidence throughout the park.

Mon Date: This is the "monumented date," or year the marker was placed, based on either the NGS datasheet or the stamping on the marker itself. In a few cases, the year has been estimated based on a marker's similarity to other markers.

Responsible Agency: This is the agency that monumented (placed) the marker, again based on information contained on NGS datasheets or information stamped on the marker. Agency codes used in these lists include:

- **BPR:** Bureau of Public Roads (FHWA's predecessor)
- **PRA/FWA:** Public Roads Admin/Federal Works Agency
- **FHWA:** Federal Highway Administration
- **USCGS:** U.S. Coast & Geodetic Survey (predecessor of NGS)
- **NGS:** National Geodetic Survey
- **USGS:** U.S. Geological Survey
- **CVO:** Cascades Volcano Observatory (USGS)
- **NPS:** National Park Service
- **USDI:** U.S. Department of the Interior
- **MHC:** Montana Highway Commission
- **GLO:** General Land Office (now known as the BLM)
- **UNAVCO/PBO**: Plate Boundary Observatory[3]

To Reach: The "To Reach" verbiage describes how to locate the marker using local landmarks such as intersections, bridges/overpasses, rock formations, pullouts, large trees, etc. The minimum amount necessary to locate the marker has been provided and is known to be accurate (this is how the markers were located for this book). If you're unable to locate it via the "To Reach" information, try the GPS coordinates, or use the book's web site to check for context photographs that will often provide visual clues as to the marker's location.

3 UNAVCO: University Navstar Consortium, a consortium of universities organized to study geosciences, primarily in the western United States.

Part III
Yellowstone Benchmark Lists

The following pages provide the lists of benchmarks along each segment of road within the park. There is also a section at the end for miscellaneous markers that are not located along one of the major road segments. The lists are in the order of travel if you were to enter the park from the North Entrance and proceed throughout the park in a clockwise fashion along the park's "Figure 8" Grand Loop Road. The list for each entrance road is setup as if you were entering the park for the first time from that road; you can pick up the remainder of the Grand Loop Road segments from its intersection with the entrance roads.

The page numbering from this point forward shifts a bit. Instead of regular page numbers, each road segment is designated by a code sequence (provided in parentheses in the list below) that identifies the road segment, plus a sequential page number. This is done to allow each section list to stand on its own, and allows for easier indexing of the PIDs (there is a full index of PIDs at the end of this book).

- North Entrance Road (NER)
- Mammoth Hot Springs to Tower Junction (MHS-TJ)
- Northeast Entrance Road (NEER)
- Tower Junction to Canyon Junction (TJ-CJ)
- Canyon Junction to Fishing Bridge (CJ-FB)
- East Entrance Road (EER)
- Fishing Bridge to West Thumb (FB-WT)
- South Entrance Road (SER)
- West Thumb to Old Fatihful (WT-OF)
- Old Faithful to Madison Junction (OF-MD)
- West Entrance Road (WER)
- Madison Junction to Norris Junction (MD-NJ)
- Norris Junction to Canyon Junction (NJ-CJ)
- Norris Junction to Mammoth Hot Springs (NJ-MHS)
- U.S. Highway 191 (US191)
- Miscellaneous Benchmarks (MISC)

Yellowstone Benchmarks
North Entrance Road

From the North: Reset your odometer/GPS at the Roosevelt Arch
From Mammoth Hot Springs: Reset your odometer/GPS as you pass the Mammoth Post Office heading north

Most of the benchmarks along this section are a mixture of those installed by the Bureau of Public Roads in 1923 and the U.S. Coast and Geodetic Survey in 1960. There's one interesting cast-iron NPS marker from an unknown date (but believed to be from the late 1910s). If you elect to go looking for the CORS station east of the old school, understand that you're entering a residential area. Park at the school and walk back to the station's location.

| PID: QX0584 | Stamp: D 565 1983 | Family: Y | Access: N | Ease: E |

Coordinates: 45.0295100 -110.70837   Elevation: 5318.45

Mon Date: 1983   Responsible Agency: NGS

To Reach: South & east of Roosevelt Arch, in 3x3 ft exposed bedrock, 76 ft E
of the center of the archway, 47 ft NE of road centerline.

| NOTES |

| PID: QX0585 | Stamp: E 565 1983 | Family: Y | Access: N | Ease: E |

Coordinates: 45.02079 -110.69647   Elevation: 5357.41

Mon Date: 1983   Responsible Agency: NGS

To Reach: 0.85 miles S of Roosevelt Arch on North Entrance Road, at SE
end of paved pullout with interpretive display on the "Northern
Range," in 3x3 ft exposed bedrock, 22 ft E of E edge of interpretive display sign

| NOTES |

| PID: QX9902 | Stamp: 19 | Family: N | Access: Y | Ease: E |

Coordinates: 45.01125 -110.69426   Elevation: 5455.00

Mon Date: 1923   Responsible Agency: BPR

To Reach: 1.65 miles S of Gardiner on North Entrance Road, in N end of E
walkway on bridge over Gardner River.

| NOTES |

| **PID: QX0116** | Stamp: G 162 1960 | Family: N | Access: N | Ease: E |

Coordinates: 45.01093 -110.69408   Elevation: 5427.03

Mon Date: 1960   Responsible Agency: USCGS

To Reach: 1.65 miles S of Gardiner on North Entrance Road, in S end of E
                 walkway on bridge over the Gardner River.

| NOTES |

| **PID: PY9906** | Stamp: 58 | Family: N | Access: Y | Ease: E |

Coordinates: 44.99341 -110.69328   Elevation: 5699.00

Mon Date: 1923   Responsible Agency: BPR

To Reach: 2.25 miles N of Mammoth Post Office, on the bridge over the
                 Gardner River. At the NW end of the W walkway of the bridge N
                 of the Boiling River turnout.

| NOTES |

| **PID: PY0155** | Stamp: J 162 1960 | Family: N | Access: N | Ease: E |

Coordinates: 44.99324 -110.69303   Elevation: 5632.89

Mon Date: 1960   Responsible Agency: USCGS

To Reach: 2.25 miles N of Mammoth Post Office, on the bridge over the
                 Gardner River. In the NW end of the W walkway of the bridge N
                 of the Boiling River turnout.

| NOTES |

| PID: PY0156 | Stamp: X 8 5631.590 | Family: N | Access: N | Ease: E |

Coordinates: 44.99235 -110.6922   **Elevation:** 5635.82

Mon Date: 1923   **Responsible Agency:** USCGS

To Reach: 2.2 miles N of Mammoth Post Office, set off E side of road, 200 ft S of the entry road for the Boiling River parking lot, on a concrete post. Requires walk down steep slope.

NOTES

| PID: PY0158 | Stamp: 15 | Family: N | Access: N | Ease: M |

Coordinates: 44.98084 -110.69174   **Elevation:** 5942.06

Mon Date: Unknown   **Responsible Agency:** NPS

To Reach: 1.25 miles N of Mammoth Post Office, 132 ft W of road center-line, 0.2 mi NE of Mammoth Campground. Green metal post next to small USDI marker. Park vehicle in gravel turnout across from Lava Creek Trailhead, and hike 420 ft N along summit of hill. You'll see the short green post out in the field to your left.

NOTES

| PID: AI5647 | Stamp: N/A | Family: N | Access: N | Ease: E |

Coordinates: 44.973447, -110.689289   **Elevation:** 5985.05

Mon Date: 1998   **Responsible Agency:** UNAVCO/PBO

To Reach: 0.9 miles N of Mammoth Post Office, turn E into residential drive, then into old school parking lot. Walk approx 300 ft E of school to earthen vault with "Seismic Station" sign on door. Station is on hill above vault.

NOTES

PID: PY0159   Stamp: B 157 1960   Family: N   Access: N   Ease: M

Coordinates: 44.972022 -110.694254   Elevation: 6062.06

Mon Date: 1960   Responsible Agency: USCGS

To Reach: 0.55 miles N of Mammoth Post Office, 58 ft from road centerline
                 inside the hairpin curve just before you enter the curve.

NOTES

PID: PY0160   Stamp: Y8 1923 6239   Family: Y   Access: Y   Ease: E

Coordinates: 44.976365971 -110.699768   Elevation: 6243.78

Mon Date: 1923   Responsible Agency: USCGS

To Reach: Located on small concrete monument right in front of Albright
                 VC next to walkway

NOTES

Yellowstone Benchmarks
Mammoth Hot Springs to Tower Junction

From Norris Junction: Reset your odometer/GPS at the intersection in front of the Mammoth Hot Springs Hotel.

From Tower Junction: Reset your odometer/GPS at the intersection in front of the entrance to the Roosevelt Lodge

Most of the benchmarks along this section of roadway are from the 1987 leveling survey undertaken by the National Geodetic Survey. There are a few remaining older ones from the 1923 surveys as well, including some that are fairly easy to get to along old road segments. There are about a dozen other benchmarks along this segment of roadway that have been left off this list, primarily because the road is so narrow and winding that it would be unsafe to stop and search for them.

PID: PY1008 Stamp: G 365 1987 Family: N Access: N Ease: M

Coordinates: 44.96983926 -110.6978086 Elevation: 6182.65

Mon Date: 1987 Responsible Agency: NGS

To Reach: 0.5 miles E of Mammoth Hot Springs Jct, on S side of road, 56 ft W of road centerline, 16 ft above roadway, in bedrock just above triple-trunked juniper tree. You'll need to park at the Mammoth Chapel parking lot and walk S to marker.

NOTES

PID: PY1009 Stamp: H 365 1987 Family: N Access: N Ease: E

Coordinates: 44.96454 -110.68783 Elevation: 6007.66

Mon Date: 1987 Responsible Agency: NGS

To Reach: 1.1 miles E of Mammoth Hot Springs Jct, just east of the large pullout on S side of road. Logo cap.

NOTES

PID: PY1010 Stamp: 5 RDS 1955 Family: N Access: N Ease: E

Coordinates: 44.957340 -110.67803 Elevation: 6071.18

Mon Date: 1955 Responsible Agency: USGS

To Reach: 1.85 miles E of Mammoth Hot Springs Jct on Gardner River Bridge, at SE corner on top of S abutment

NOTES

PID: PY0153   **Stamp: Z 11 1923**   **Family: N**   **Access: N**   **Ease: D**

Coordinates: 44.94446 -110.64307   **Elevation: 6674.49**

Mon Date: 1923   **Responsible Agency: USCGS**

To Reach: 4.1 miles E of Mammoth Hot Springs Jct to Undine Falls parking area, 50 ft S of existing road, 60 ft above existing road on old dirt road/trail, 650 ft W up old roadbed (may be hard to discern during the summer), on a brown stone post.

NOTES

PID: PY1015   **Stamp: 6558.70 1934**   **Family: N**   **Access: N**   **Ease: E**

Coordinates: 44.94078 -110.63233   **Elevation: 6563.59**

Mon Date: 1934   **Responsible Agency: BPR**

To Reach: 4.4 miles E of Mammoth Hot Springs Jct, on south side of bridge over Lava Creek at the Lava Creek Picnic Area, behind guard rail on west end.

NOTES

PID: PY0152   **Stamp: Y 11 1923**   **Family: N**   **Access: N**   **Ease: M**

Coordinates: 44.94793 -110.61433   **Elevation: 6654.85**

Mon Date: 1923   **Responsible Agency: USCGS**

To Reach: 5.4 miles E of Mammoth Hot Springs Jct, first gavel pullout (5.6 miles) on N side of road E of Wraith Falls Trailhead, set in top of 5 ft boulder . Hike back W about 500 ft from pullout along road (be careful of traffic!)

NOTES

PID: PY1016 Stamp: 10-19 1986   Family: N   Access: N   Ease: E

Coordinates: 44.9501 -110.61183   Elevation: 6657.02

Mon Date: 1986   Responsible Agency: FHWA

To Reach: 5.7 miles E of Mammoth Hot Springs Jct, across & up the road
(east) from PY0152 at first pullout west of Blacktail Lakes, 54 ft N
of road centerline on other side of slight hill, 4.5 ft NW of metal
fence post.

NOTES

PID: PY1017 Stamp: M 365 1987   Family: N   Access: N   Ease: M

Coordinates: 44.95252 -110.60378   Elevation: 6664

Mon Date: 1987   Responsible Agency: NGS

To Reach: 6.2 miles E of Mammoth Hot Springs Jct, across highway from
W end of Blacktail Pond, 235 ft S of sign @ W end of highway
pullout, 50 ft S of road centerline on top of 3x6 rock (possibly with
a tree stump lying over it).

NOTES

PID: PY1018 Stamp: N 365 1987   Family: N   Access: N   Ease: E

Coordinates: 44.95541 -110.59391   Elevation: 6641.20

Mon Date: 1987   Responsible Agency: NGS

To Reach: 6.7 miles E of Mammoth Hot Springs Jct, 78 ft W of center of
Blacktail Deer Trail, embedded in bedrock, 22 ft N of road centerline.

NOTES

| **PID: PY1020** | Stamp: 4 RDS 1955 | Family: N | Access: N | Ease: M |

Coordinates: 44.95980546 -110.5655589   **Elevation: 6938.50**

Mon Date: 1955   **Responsible Agency: USGS**

To Reach: 8.35 miles E of Mammoth Hot Springs Jct, E of Children's Fire Trail parking area, 134 ft NE of NE end of pullout, 34 ft N of road centerline.

NOTES

| **PID: PY0151** | Stamp: N/A | Family: N | Access: N | Ease: M |

Coordinates: 44.95788 -110.5667   **Elevation: 6917.60**

Mon Date: 1923   **Responsible Agency: USCGS**

To Reach: 8.35 miles E of Mammoth Hot Springs Jct, park in Frog Rock Service Road entrance, look to the southwest for old road bed, then travel 400 ft west to monument in large boulder on S side of old road.

NOTES

| **PID: PY1022** | Stamp: Q 365 1987 | Family: N | Access: N | Ease: E |

Coordinates: 44.95792 -110.54158   **Elevation: 6910.34**

Mon Date: 1987   **Responsible Agency: NGS**

To Reach: 9.55 miles E of Mammoth Hot Springs Jct, @ entrance to Blacktail Plateau Drive, SE of intersection, 21 ft E of Blacktail Plateau Drive, 61 ft S of main road centerline.

NOTES

PID: PY0150   Stamp: HARDROCK   Family: N   Access: N   Ease: M

Coordinates: 44.94894 -110.51519   Elevation: 7195.33

Mon Date: 1987   Responsible Agency: NGS

To Reach: 9.55 miles E of Mammoth Hot Springs Jct, then 1.7 miles E on
                 Blacktail Plateau Drive, 30 ft N of road, in boulder near metal util-
                 ity box. Listed in NGS database as "W 11."

NOTES

PID: PY1023   Stamp: T 365 1987   Family: N   Access: N   Ease: M

Coordinates: 44.9553 -110.5291   Elevation: 6791.25

Mon Date: 1987   Responsible Agency: NGS

To Reach: 7.9 miles W of Tower Ranger Sta, @ Phantom Lake pullout, 20 ft
                 behind 2nd large boulder from the west end of pullout. Logo cap

NOTES

PID: PY1028   Stamp: W 365 1987   Family: N   Access: N   Ease: E

Coordinates: 44.94856 -110.46873   Elevation: 6654.45

Mon Date: 1987   Responsible Agency: NGS

To Reach: 4.4 miles W of Tower Jct, 49 ft W of center of paved pullout, on N
                 side of highway, 30 ft N of road centerline. Logo cap

NOTES

PID: PY1029   Stamp: V 365 1987   Family: N   Access: N   Ease: M

Coordinates: 44.9484138 -110.45333   Elevation: 6570.09

Mon Date: 1987   Responsible Agency: NGS

To Reach: 3.65 miles W of Tower Jct, 0.05 miles N on Hellroaring Trailhead Road, at highest point of rock outcrop on E side of road, 110 ft E of road centerline, 22 ft above road surface level

NOTES

PID: PY1035   Stamp: NO 2   Family: N   Access: N   Ease: E

Coordinates: 44.91651 -110.41817   Elevation: 6274.39

Mon Date: 1923   Responsible Agency: USCGS

To Reach: 0.1 miles W of Tower Jct, 212 ft N of Service Station, just W of W entrance to station parking lot, 65 ft SW of road centerline, at top of small hill, on concrete pedestal

NOTES

Yellowstone Benchmarks
Northeast Entrance Road

From Tower Junction: Reset your odometer/GPS at the intersection just as you get ready to turn onto the Northeast Entrance Road
From Northeast Gate: Reset your odometer/GPS as you sit at the Northeast Entrance Station ranger window.

Most of the benchmarks along this stretch of roadway were installed in 1941 by the Public Roads Administration of the Federal Works Agency, an entity created during the Great Depression to foster public roads projects as a means of putting people to work. This stretch of roadway is one of only three in the park where you'll find markers with the stampings of this agency (it only existed for ten years). Though the USGS did some work along this road in 1936 and 1941, many of its markers no longer survive. The balance of the markers are from the 1987 leveling surveys undertaken by the National Geodetic Survey.

| PID: PY1036 | Stamp: X 365 1987 | Family: N | Access: N | Ease: E |

Coordinates: 44.916170 -110.41582   Elevation: 6269.48

Mon Date: 1987   Responsible Agency: USCGS

To Reach: At Tower Jct, just 1.5 ft W of leg of directional sign intended for traffic approaching the junction on the NE Entrance Road. Logo cap

| NOTES |

| PID: PY1037 | Stamp: 12-1 1986 | Family: N | Access: N | Ease: E |

Coordinates: 44.91941 -110.41191   Elevation: 6236.20

Mon Date: 1986   Responsible Agency: FHWA

To Reach: 0.35 miles NE of Tower Jct, on small hill E of roadway, 43 ft N of horse trail, 3 ft from metal post.

| NOTES |

| PID: PY1038 | Stamp: 19 | Family: N | Access: N | Ease: E |

Coordinates: 44.92022 -110.40567   Elevation: 6095.13

Mon Date: 1961   Responsible Agency: BPR

To Reach: 0.6 miles NE of Tower Jct, on NW corner walkway of Yellowstone River Bridge. May be covered by dirt/debris

| NOTES |

| PID: PY1039 | Stamp: DWU | Family: N | Access: N | Ease: E |

Coordinates: 44.920430 -110.40336   **Elevation:** 6091.39

Mon Date: 1961   **Responsible Agency:** BPR

To Reach: 0.7 miles E of Tower Jct, in NE end of N walkway of bridge over Yellowstone River. May be covered by dirt/debris

NOTES

| PID: PY1077 | Stamp: VS 41 1936 | Family: N | Access: N | Ease: D |

Coordinates: 44.91402 -110.39198   **Elevation:** 6262.85

Mon Date: 1936   **Responsible Agency:** USGS

To Reach: 1.7 miles NE of Tower Jct, in center of large, dome-shaped boulder, on NE edge of small pond (may be wet and reachable only late in the season), 246 ft N of road centerline.

NOTES

| PID: PY1043 | Stamp: 18 MDC 1977 | Family: N | Access: N | Ease: E |

Coordinates: 44.90745 -110.34264   **Elevation:** 6227.58

Mon Date: 1977   **Responsible Agency:** USGS

To Reach: 4.25 miles NE of Tower Jct, on culvert headwall across the road and 50 ft NE of paved pullout, 20 ft N of road centerline

NOTES

PID: PY1078	Stamp: 6449.66	Family: N	Access: N	Ease: D

Coordinates: 44.9186 -110.29405   Elevation: 6456.01

Mon Date: 1941   Responsible Agency: PRA/FWA

To Reach: 7.0 miles NE of Tower Jct, 66 ft SW of road centerline, S side of road halfway between pullouts (park in easternmost & walk back W), in E side of 6x6 boulder above and alongside the river. Be careful of traffic. Will require climb onto 4 ft rock

NOTES

PID: PY1049	Stamp: 6626.42 8 2	Family: N	Access: N	Ease: M

Coordinates: 44.91241 -110.25958   Elevation: 6632.89

Mon Date: 1941   Responsible Agency: PRA/FWA

To Reach: 8.75 miles NE of Tower Jct, on headwall of stone culvert on north side of road, 42 ft SW of pullout (across road)

NOTES

PID: PY1051	Stamp: 12-4 1986	Family: N	Access: N	Ease: E

Coordinates: 44.89433 -110.2354   Elevation: 6550.43

Mon Date: 1986   Responsible Agency: FHWA

To Reach: 10.5 miles NE of Tower Jct, 26 ft SE of interpretive sign at pullout across from Buffalo Ranch. 3 ft from metal post

NOTES

PID: PY1052   **Stamp: Z 368 1987**   **Family: N**   **Access: N**   **Ease: E**

Coordinates: 44.89515 -110.23457   **Elevation:** 6571.91

Mon Date: 1987   **Responsible Agency:** NGS

To Reach: 10.5 miles NE of Tower Jct, at Buffalo Ranch, 6 ft W/NW of S corner of the barn, 3 ft SW of the S corner of the barn. Logo cap. May be under stored materials

NOTES

PID: PY1053   **Stamp: 6552.22 8 2**   **Family: N**   **Access: N**   **Ease: M**

Coordinates: 44.89365 -110.23398   **Elevation:** 6558.71

Mon Date: 1941   **Responsible Agency:** PRA/FWA

To Reach: 10.6 miles NE of Tower Jct, N side of road, in center of NE headwall of culvert, 0.1 mile SE of Buffalo Ranch access road

NOTES

PID: PY1055   **Stamp: 6570.59 8 2**   **Family: N**   **Access: N**   **Ease: E**

Coordinates: 44.87111 -110.20467   **Elevation:** 6577.21

Mon Date: 1941   **Responsible Agency:** PRA/FWA

To Reach: 12.7 miles NE of Tower Jct, between two unpaved pullouts, on top of culvert headwall

NOTES

PID: PY1058   Stamp: 6619.26 8 2   **Family: N**   **Access: N**   **Ease: E**

Coordinates: 44.86851 -110.1734   **Elevation: 6625.78**

Mon Date: 1941   **Responsible Agency: PRA/FWA**

To Reach: 14.2 miles NE of Tower Jct, in center of culvert headwall on N side of road 66 ft E of Lamar River Stock Trailhead parking area

NOTES

PID: PY1059   Stamp: 4 GWM 1941   **Family: N**   **Access: N**   **Ease: E**

Coordinates: 44.87288 -110.16193   **Elevation: 6652.61**

Mon Date: 1941   **Responsible Agency: USGS**

To Reach: 13.0 miles SW of Northeast Ent Sta, on top of headwall of stone culvert 38 ft SE of small gravel pullout, 20 ft SE of road centerline

NOTES

PID: PY1060   Stamp: 6652.02 8 1   **Family: N**   **Access: N**   **Ease: E**

Coordinates: 44.87856 -110.15234   **Elevation: 6658.51**

Mon Date: 1941   **Responsible Agency: PRA/FWA**

To Reach: 12.4 miles SW of Northeast Entrance Station, on north side of road, 220 ft NE of Soda Butte, on headwall of stone culvert.

NOTES

PID: PY1063 Stamp: 6738.91 8 1   Family: N   Access: N   Ease: M

Coordinates: 44.89791 -110.12437   Elevation: 6745.42

Mon Date: 1941   Responsible Agency: PRA/FWA

To Reach: 17.55 miles NE of Tower Jct, 400 ft S of Trout Lake Trailhead, on
                 north side of road just below roadway, 4 feet off road on culvert
                 headwall.

NOTES

PID: PY1067 Stamp: 6835.25 8 1   Family: N   Access: N   Ease: E

Coordinates: 44.91484 -110.11234   Elevation: 6841.74

Mon Date: 1941   Responsible Agency: PRA/FWA

To Reach: 9.15 miles SW of Northeast Entrance Station, NW side of Pebble
                 Creek Bridge behind 3rd post from the west. Park in Pebble Creek
                 Campground entrance lot & walk to bridge

NOTES

PID: PY1069 Stamp: 6902.10 8 1   Family: N   Access: N   Ease: M

Coordinates: 44.92102 -110.09687   Elevation: 6907.62

Mon Date: 1941   Responsible Agency: PRA/FWA

To Reach: 8.25 miles SW of Northeast Entrance Station, center of NW
                 headwall of culvert, 200 ft SW of SW end of trailhead parking
                 area, across road from "Thunderer" sign for NE bound traffic.

NOTES

PID: PY1071   Stamp: X 368 1987   Family: N   Access: N   Ease: M

Coordinates: 44.93501 -110.08404   Elevation: 6963.68

Mon Date: 1987   Responsible Agency: NGS

To Reach: 7.1 miles SW of Northeast Entrance Station, across from parking
              area, 24 ft W of road centerline, 92 ft S of picnic area's northeast
              entry

NOTES

PID: PY1072   Stamp: 7008.17 8 1   Family: N   Access: N   Ease: E

Coordinates: 44.94497 -110.08243   Elevation: 7014.65

Mon Date: 1941   Responsible Agency: PRA/FWA

To Reach: 6.35 miles SW of Northeast Entrance Station, on bridge over Soda
              Butte Creek, 5th post from the south end on west side of bridge.

NOTES

PID: PY1074   Stamp: 7171.69 8 1   Family: N   Access: N   Ease: E

Coordinates: 44.96809 -110.06921   Elevation: 7178.270

Mon Date: 1941   Responsible Agency: PRA/FWA

To Reach: 4.65 miles SW of Northeast Entrance Station, in SW wall of
              bridge over dry wash, not on bridge, but on wing wall behind it.
              No pullout at the bridge. Use caution.

NOTES

PID: PY1125   Stamp: 7194.05   Family: N   Access: N   Ease: E

Coordinates: 44.99131 -110.05668   Elevation: 7200.56

Mon Date: 1941   Responsible Agency: PRA/FWA

To Reach: 2.8 miles SW of Northeast Ent Sta, in concrete bridge over Soda
                 Butte Creek, S end of west wing. Park in turnout W of bridge &
                 walk back.

NOTES

PID: QX0622   Stamp: 7348.85   Family: N   Access: Y   Ease: E

Coordinates: 45.004709 -110.009712   Elevation: 7355.42

Mon Date: 1941   Responsible Agency: PRA/FWA

To Reach: At Northeast Entrance Station, 85 ft E of station, 30 ft N of high-
                 way centerline, on top of masonry culvert

NOTES

Yellowstone Benchmarks
Tower Junction to Canyon Junction

From Tower Junction: Reset your odometer/GPS at the intersection in front of the entrance to the Roosevelt Lodge
From Canyon Junction: Reset your odometer/GPS at the intersection

Most of the original 1923 benchmarks installed along this road are gone, having been plowed over during its reconstruction in the mid-2000s. The only two remaining are one in the Tower Campground (near the northern end of the original road through this area) and the one at the top of Chittenden Road at its switchback into the parking area. For many years, it was possible to drive up one side of Mt. Washburn and down the other via what is now Chittenden Road. Today, you can drive part of the way up, and then hike three miles to the Fire Lookout atop the mountain. At the summit of Mt. Washburn can be found the three most popular benchmarks in the park. The balance of the markers along the road are from the mid-1970s, and from the 1987 leveling survey done by the NGS.

PID: PY0979   Stamp: 17 MDC 1977   Family: N   Access: N   Ease: M

Coordinates: 44.91416 -110.41084   Elevation: 6282.38

Mon Date: 1977   Responsible Agency: USGS

To Reach: 0.3 miles E of Tower Jct, on top of 8x12 boulder in a clump of
                 trees, 78 ft S/SW of of road centerline, 90 ft NW of the NW end
                 of pullout for Roosevelt Corral Service Road.

NOTES

PID: PY0981   Stamp: 16 MDC 1977   Family: Y   Access: N   Ease: E

Coordinates: 44.90173 -110.39339   Elevation: 6523.06

Mon Date: 1977   Responsible Agency: USGS

To Reach: 1.3 miles E of Tower Jct, across the road from the Calcite Springs
                 Overlook parking lot, in 6x8 ft boulder. Marker S 11 (PY0028) is a
                 few feet southwest of this one)

NOTES

PID: PY0982   Stamp: C 366 1987   Family: N   Access: N   Ease: M

Coordinates: 44.89235 -110.38799   Elevation: 6451.63

Mon Date: 1987   Responsible Agency: NGS

To Reach: 2.3 miles E of Tower Jct, on 2x4 rock ledge, 12 ft NW of the south-
                 west guardrail of the bridge over Tower Creek. May be covered by
                 dirt/debris

NOTES

PID: PY0027 Stamp: R 11 1923 6597   Family: N   Access: Y   Ease: E

Coordinates: 44.8899397 -110.3897955   Elevation: 6602.52

Mon Date: 1923   Responsible Agency: USCGS

To Reach: 2.35 miles E of Tower Jct, in Tower Fall Campground, drive down Campground entrance road to 3-way (past 4-way), S of main road, 5ft above road, on large boulder near fire pit and food storage bin # 8

NOTES

PID: PY0984 Stamp: 21 MDC 1976   Family: N   Access: Y   Ease: E

Coordinates: 44.87358 -110.38209   Elevation: 7639.12

Mon Date: 1976   Responsible Agency: USGS

To Reach: 3.7 miles SE of Tower Jct, in 4x4 boulder that projects 24" out of ground, in pullout on E side of road. 33 ft SE of "Antelope Creek" sign, & 3 ft N of FHWY sign

NOTES

PID: PY0987 Stamp: F 366 1987   Family: N   Access: N   Ease: E

Coordinates: 44.859354 -110.40949   Elevation: 7483.41

Mon Date: 1987   Responsible Agency: NGS

To Reach: 6.05 miles E of Tower Jct, 47 ft W of road centerline immediately west of pullout on east side of hwy, 3 ft S of sign post. Logo cap, may be covered by dirt

NOTES

PID: PY0988   Stamp: 19 MDC 1976   Family: N   Access: N   Ease: E

Coordinates: 44.85329 -110.41676   Elevation: 7667.38

Mon Date: 1976   Responsible Agency: USGS

To Reach: 6.7 miles E of Tower Jct, on top of 8x8 boulder on east end of pull-out on south side of road, projecting 40" out of ground.

NOTES

PID: PY0991   Stamp: J 366 1987   Family: N   Access: Y   Ease: M

Coordinates: 44.8401 -110.43705   Elevation: 8094.97

Mon Date: 1987   Responsible Agency: NGS

To Reach: 8.15 miles SE of Tower Jct, on north side of Mae West Curve (hairpin curve north of Chittenden Rd), 50 ft N of the S end of small dirt pullout N of the curve itself, 26 ft E of road centerline

NOTES

PID: PY1215   Stamp: WASHBURN   Family: Y   Access: N   Ease: D

Coordinates: 44.797716 -110.433887   Elevation: 10249.00

Mon Date: 1950   Responsible Agency: USCGS

To Reach: 9.7 miles N of Canyon Jct, 1.3 miles S on Chittenden Rd, then walk 3.0 miles to summit. Azimuth Mark at summit of Mt. Washburn, 2 ft from log side rail on N arc of summit pad. Full stamp reads: WASHBURN 1950

NOTES

| PID: CQ7584 | Stamp: WASHBURN 1 | Family: Y | Access: N | Ease: D |

Coordinates: 44.797697 -110.433777   **Elevation:** 10249.00

Mon Date: 1950   **Responsible Agency:** USCGS

To Reach: 9.7 miles N of Canyon Jct, 1.3 miles S on Chittenden Rd, then walk 3.0 miles to summit. Summit of Mt. Washburn, approximately 10 ft from Mt. Washburn Elevation sign, 68 ft N of the NE corner of the Lookout Tower. Full stamp reads: WASHBURN NO 1

NOTES

| PID: CQ7585 | Stamp: WASHBURN 2 | Family: Y | Access: N | Ease: D |

Coordinates: 44.797492 -110.433849   **Elevation:** 10249.00

Mon Date: 1950   **Responsible Agency:** USCGS

To Reach: 9.7 miles N of Canyon Jct, 1.3 miles S on Chittenden Rd, then walk 3.0 miles to summit. Summit of Mt. Washburn on septic tank concrete pad 5 ft N of the N side of Lookout Tower. Full stamp reads: WASHBURN NO 2

NOTES

| PID: PY0024 | Stamp: O 11 1923 | Family: Y | Access: N | Ease: E |

Coordinates: 44.823839 -110.445670   **Elevation:** 8757.68

Mon Date: 1923   **Responsible Agency:** USCGS

To Reach: 9.7 miles N of Canyon Jct, then 1.5 miles up Chittenden Rd, @ the switchback at the top of the Chittenden Rd where it becomes a service road, protected by three red posts

NOTES

PID: PY9915   Stamp: 18 MDC RESE   Family: N   Access: N   Ease: E

Coordinates: 44.83199669 -110.4465991   Elevation: 8405.10

Mon Date: 2002   Responsible Agency: USGS

To Reach: 9.0 miles N of Canyon Jct, W side of road 10 ft N of gravel pullout, set in rock flush with the ground about 4 ft below road surface. Marker is on the edge of a closed bear management area. Do not travel beyond the marker. Full stamp reads: 18 MDC RESET

NOTES

PID: PY1002   Stamp: 14 MDC 1976   Family: N   Access: N   Ease: E

Coordinates: 44.77678 -110.4593   Elevation: 8732.29

Mon Date: 1976   Responsible Agency: USGS

To Reach: 4.2 miles N of Canyon Jct, 68 ft SE of the N end of the pullout, 51 ft E of road centerline

NOTES

PID: PY1006   Stamp: T 366 1987   Family: N   Access: N   Ease: E

Coordinates: 44.76198868 -110.47118   Elevation: 8343.00

Mon Date: 1987   Responsible Agency: NGS

To Reach: 2.5 miles N of Canyon Jct, 55 ft NW of road centerline, 27 ft NE of centerline of entrance into Dunraven Road Picnic Area. Logo cap

NOTES

PID: PY1255	Stamp: OBSV PEAK	Family: N	Access: N	Ease: D

Coordinates: 44.772026 -110.547916   **Elevation:** 9402.00

Mon Date: 1955   **Responsible Agency:** USGS

To Reach: 1.3 miles N of Canyon Jct. Park at Cascade Lake Trailhead and hike to Cascade Lake. Take trail to Observation Peak (5.5 miles total one way). At summit of Observation Peak, on boulder 46ft W of lookout tower. Full stamp reads: OBSERVATION PEAK

NOTES

Yellowstone Benchmarks
Canyon Junction to Fishing Bridge

From Canyon Junction: Reset your odometer/GPS at the intersection
From Fishing Bridge: Reset your odometer/GPS in the middle of the intersection, or just as you enter the turning lane to go north if you're coming off the East Entrance Road

The section of roadway between Canyon Village and Fishing Bridge is perhaps the most densely populated area of the park in terms of benchmarks; there are almost three dozen markers along its 15+ miles. And those are just the ones that could be accounted for. There are records of another two dozen or so that were not located or that were deemed unsafe for the average hunter.

This is the area that has shown the most significant rise and fall over the past 90 years or so, especially along its southern half. As a result, the vast majority of markers you'll find in this section are from the ground deformation studies conducted in the 1970s and 1980s, though you will find a few of the markers the Bureau of Public Roads installed in 1934. There's also an interesting benchmark from 1923 to be found along a short section of abandoned road a couple of miles north of Fishing Bridge.

PID: PY0832 Stamp: CVO 85-230   Family: N   Access: N   Ease: E

Coordinates: 44.7271100 -110.49397   Elevation: 7922.68

Mon Date: 1985   Responsible Agency: CVO

To Reach: 0.6 miles S of Canyon Jct, @ pullout, 28 ft W of road centerline, on
              4x6 boulder, 3ft above ground

NOTES

PID: PY0833 Stamp: HOLLIS   Family: N   Access: N   Ease: E

Coordinates: 44.7226700 -110.4948700   Elevation: 7957.28

Mon Date: 1987   Responsible Agency: NGS

To Reach: 0.9 miles S of Canyon Jct, 150 ft SW of the centerline of Canyon
              Corral Road, 43 ft W of highway centerline on small hill, 9 ft above
              road level, in 3x6 boulder projecting 24" from ground

NOTES

PID: PY0834 Stamp: LC 58 1977   Family: N   Access: N   Ease: E

Coordinates: 44.7167900 -110.50528   Elevation: 7767.70

Mon Date: 1977   Responsible Agency: NPS

To Reach: 1.6 miles S of Canyon Jct, top of 4x6 domed rock outcropping, 98
              ft W of road centerline, 30 ft N of Canyon Electrical Substation
              Service Road centerline, just NE of barricade gate

NOTES

PID: PY9917 | **Stamp: LC 57 1977**   **Family: N**   **Access: N**   **Ease: M**

Coordinates: 44.7016100 -110.5099600   **Elevation: 7754.00**

Mon Date: 1977   **Responsible Agency: NPS**

To Reach: 2.6 miles S of Canyon Jct, then hiking W on the old Otter Creek
Service Road. Marker is located next to a metal post in field on a
hill just NE of Otter Creek Bridge.

NOTES

PID: PY9916 | **Stamp: LC 54 1977**   **Family: N**   **Access: N**   **Ease: M**

Coordinates: 44.6995700 -110.51105   **Elevation: 7738.00**

Mon Date: 1977   **Responsible Agency: NPS**

To Reach: 2.6 miles S of Canyon Jct, then hiking W on the old Otter Creek
Service Road. Marker is located on S side of bridge over Otter
Creek.

NOTES

PID: PY0836 | **Stamp: Y 367 1987**   **Family: N**   **Access: N**   **Ease: E**

Coordinates: 44.70266 -110.50546   **Elevation: 7676.70**

Mon Date: 1987   **Responsible Agency: NGS**

To Reach: 2.65 miles S of Canyon Jct, in bedrock 379 ft N of the NE corner
of the bridge spanning Otter Creek, at edge of Yellowstone River,
36 ft E of road centerline. May be under water during high water
periods.

NOTES

PID: PY0837   **Stamp: 23 MDC 1976**   **Family: N**   **Access: N**   **Ease: E**

Coordinates: 44.70164 -110.50616   **Elevation: 7683.82**

Mon Date: 1976   **Responsible Agency: USGS**

To Reach: 2.75 miles S of Canyon Jct, on the S end of the W side of the bridge over Otter Creek

NOTES

PID: PY0841   **Stamp: Z 367 1987**   **Family: N**   **Access: N**   **Ease: E**

Coordinates: 44.6792900 -110.48876   **Elevation: 7692.85**

Mon Date: 1987   **Responsible Agency: NGS**

To Reach: 4.6 miles S of Canyon Jct, N of Alum Creek, at highway pullout on W side of road, 62 ft W of road centerline. Logo cap

NOTES

PID: PY0842   **Stamp: 25 MDC 1976**   **Family: N**   **Access: N**   **Ease: E**

Coordinates: 44.677612 -110.48582   **Elevation: 7780.16**

Mon Date: 1976   **Responsible Agency: USGS**

To Reach: 4.75 miles S of Canyon Jct, in E headwall of stone culvert over Alum Creek

NOTES

PID: PY0843 **Stamp: CVO 84-3**   **Family: N**   **Access: N**   **Ease: E**

Coordinates: 44.67387 -110.47964   **Elevation: 7686.27**

Mon Date: 1984   **Responsible Agency: CVO**

To Reach: 5.15 miles S of Canyon Jct, on headwall of culvert over stream (down slope on S side of road), 29 ft SW of road centerline, 5 Ft SE of PY0844.

NOTES

PID: PY0844 **Stamp: CVO 85-228**   **Family: N**   **Access: N**   **Ease: E**

Coordinates: 44.6739 -110.47968   **Elevation: 7686.33**

Mon Date: 1985   **Responsible Agency: CVO**

To Reach: 5.15 miles S of Canyon Jct, on headwall of culvert over stream (down slope on side of road), 26 ft SW of road centerline, 5ft NW of PY0843.

NOTES

PID: PY0875 **Stamp: 10-27 1986**   **Family: N**   **Access: N**   **Ease: E**

Coordinates: 44.67014 -110.47159   **Elevation: 7792.13**

Mon Date: 1986   **Responsible Agency: FHWA**

To Reach: 5.6 miles S of Canyon Jct, 77 ft east of road centerline at crest of small hill NNW of Grizzly Overlook.

NOTES

PID: PY0846 | Stamp: CVO 84-6   Family: N   Access: N   Ease: E

Coordinates: 44.669445 -110.47126   Elevation: 7780.26

Mon Date: 1984   Responsible Agency: CVO

To Reach: 5.65 miles S of Canyon Jct, in stone culvert on W side of road just N of Grizzly Overlook, 17 ft west of road centerline, 5 ft SE of PY0845

NOTES

PID: PY0845 | Stamp: CVO 85-227   Family: N   Access: N   Ease: E

Coordinates: 44.669445 -110.47125   Elevation: 7780.46

Mon Date: 1985   Responsible Agency: CVO

To Reach: 5.65 miles S of Canyon Jct, on headwall of stone culvert on W side of road just N of Grizzly Overlook, 6.5 ft SE of fiberglass stake.

NOTES

PID: PY0847 | Stamp: CVO 84-4   Family: N   Access: N   Ease: E

Coordinates: 44.66357 -110.4649   Elevation: 7699.08

Mon Date: 1984   Responsible Agency: CVO

To Reach: 6.1 miles S of Canyon Jct, on stone culvert 16 ft W of road centerline

NOTES

| **PID: PY0848** | Stamp: CVO 85-226 | Family: N | Access: N | Ease: E |

Coordinates: 44.66359 -110.46495   Elevation: 7698.99

Mon Date: 1985   Responsible Agency: CVO

To Reach: 6.1 miles S of Canyon Jct, on stone culvert 16 ft W of road center-line, 125 ft N of pullout

NOTES

| **PID: PY0901** | Stamp: KAYGEE | Family: N | Access: N | Ease: E |

Coordinates: 44.66285 -110.46405   Elevation: 7786.72

Mon Date: 1987   Responsible Agency: NGS

To Reach: 6.15 miles S of Canyon Jct, @ pullout on E side of road, 110 ft E of road centerline, in 10x25 ft bedrock, 76 ft NE of E end of drainpipe

NOTES

| **PID: PY0851** | Stamp: CVO 84-5 | Family: N | Access: N | Ease: M |

Coordinates: 44.65398 -110.46433   Elevation: 7692.94

Mon Date: 1984   Responsible Agency: CVO

To Reach: 6.8 miles S of Canyon Jct, on stone culvert, 16 ft W of road center-line, near brown fiberglass stake. 320 ft S of pullout

NOTES

PID: PY0016   Stamp: F-11 A 1934   Family: N   Access: N   Ease: E

Coordinates: 44.64599 -110.45861   Elevation: 7694.38

Mon Date: 1934   Responsible Agency: USCGS

To Reach: 7.5 miles S of Canyon Jct, on the northeast headwall of the culvert
over Trout Creek in Hayden Valley. Requires walk alongside edge
of road. Watch traffic

NOTES

PID: PY0015   Stamp: E11 A2 1934   Family: N   Access: N   Ease: E

Coordinates: 44.64058 -110.45492   Elevation: 7698.57

Mon Date: 1934   Responsible Agency: USCGS

To Reach: 7.95 miles S of Canyon Jct, on the northeast headwall of the culvert
over Elk Antler Creek in Hayden Valley. Requires walk alongside
edge of road. Watch traffic

NOTES

PID: PY0854   Stamp: CVO 85-224   Family: N   Access: N   Ease: E

Coordinates: 44.63412 -110.44767   Elevation: 7779.48

Mon Date: 1985   Responsible Agency: CVO

To Reach: 6.9 miles N of Fishing Bridge Jct, SW of wildlife turnout, on stone
culvert on W side of road. Near PY0853

NOTES

| PID: PY0853 | Stamp: CVO 84-7 | Family: N | Access: N | Ease: M |

Coordinates: 44.6341600 -110.44766   Elevation: 7779.35

Mon Date: 1984   Responsible Agency: CVO

To Reach: 6.9 miles N of Fishing Bridge Jct, SW of wildlife turnout, on stone culvert on W side of road. May be hidden by dirt/debris

NOTES

| PID: PY0855 | Stamp: 26 MDC 1976 | Family: Y | Access: Y | Ease: E |

Coordinates: 44.63053 -110.4393   Elevation: 7762.22

Mon Date: 1976   Responsible Agency: USGS

To Reach: 6.4 miles N of Fishing Bridge Jct next to Hayden Valley exhibit sign, encircled in green PVC pipe

NOTES

| PID: PY0856 | Stamp: ARBEE 1987 | Family: N | Access: N | Ease: E |

Coordinates: 44.63066 -110.43917   Elevation: 7826.08

Mon Date: 1987   Responsible Agency: NGS

To Reach: 6.4 miles N of Fishing Bridge Jct, 53 ft N/NE of (behind) the "Hayden Valley" interpretive sign, 6 ft below grade. Logo cap (broken)

NOTES

PID: PY0857   Stamp: CVO 84 22   Family: N   Access: N   Ease: E

Coordinates: 44.6301 -110.43872   Elevation: 7759.72

Mon Date: 1984   Responsible Agency: CVO

To Reach: 6.35 miles N of Fishing Bridge Jct, on stone culvert on the S side of road, across and SW of Hayden Valley Exhibit sign. May be covered by dirt

NOTES

PID: PY0860   Stamp: 27 MDC 1976   Family: N   Access: Y   Ease: E

Coordinates: 44.61845 -110.42094   Elevation: 7719.16

Mon Date: 1976   Responsible Agency: USGS

To Reach: 5.05 miles N of Fishing Bridge Jct, 36 ft NE of centerline of junction with road into Nez Perce Ford Picnic Area, encircled in green PVC pipe, possibly with gray cover on it.

NOTES

PID: PY0863   Stamp: 28 MDC 1976   Family: N   Access: N   Ease: E

Coordinates: 44.6093600 -110.39993   Elevation: 7745.48

Mon Date: 1976   Responsible Agency: USGS

To Reach: 3.8 miles N of Fishing Bridge Jct, 17 ft NW of W end of paved pullout, 33 ft N of road centerline, encircled in green PVC pipe (possibly w/ gray cover on it) in clump of trees

NOTES

PID: PY0014   **Stamp: DA3 1934 7718**   **Family: N**   **Access: N**   **Ease: M**

Coordinates: 44.60788000 -110.38839   **Elevation: 7725.92**

Mon Date: 1934   **Responsible Agency: USCGS**

To Reach: 3.15 miles N of Fishing Bridge Jct, 43 ft W of stone headwall, 40 ft S of road centerline, 125 ft W of sign "LeHardy Rapids" for southbound traffic, in concrete post

NOTES

PID: PY0864   **Stamp: 29 MDC 1976**   **Family: N**   **Access: Y**   **Ease: E**

Coordinates: 44.60516 -110.38354   **Elevation: 7776.66**

Mon Date: 1976   **Responsible Agency: USGS**

To Reach: 2.85 miles N of Fishing Bridge Jct, S of the S end of the parking area for LeHardy Rapids, 33 ft E of road centerline, encircled in green PVC pipe with a gray cover on it

NOTES

PID: PY0865   **Stamp: LEHARDY**   **Family: N**   **Access: N**   **Ease: M**

Coordinates: 44.59946 -110.38678   **Elevation: 7878.56**

Mon Date: 1987   **Responsible Agency: NGS**

To Reach: 2.4 miles N of Fishing Bridge Jct, 99 ft E of road centerline, 49 ft E of pullout curb, 52 ft SE of garbage can pedestal (concrete pad & post remain, but can is gone). Logo cap. May be covered by high grass/dirt

NOTES

PID: PY0867   Stamp: CVO 85-221   Family: N   Access: N   Ease: E

Coordinates: 44.59892 -110.38735   Elevation: 7757.45

Mon Date: 1985   Responsible Agency: CVO

To Reach: 2.35 miles N of Fishing Bridge Jct, in headwall of stone culvert, 65 ft SW of S end of pullout, 20 ft W of road centerline, near PY0866

NOTES

PID: PY0866   Stamp: CVO 84-10   Family: N   Access: N   Ease: E

Coordinates: 44.5989 -110.38737   Elevation: 7757.24

Mon Date: 1984   Responsible Agency: CVO

To Reach: 2.35 miles N of Fishing Bridge Jct, in headwall of stone culvert, 65 ft SW of S end of pullout, 20 ft W of road centerline

NOTES

PID: PY9919   Stamp: 10-29   Family: N   Access: N   Ease: E

Coordinates: 44.59501 -110.38779   Elevation: 7790.00

Mon Date: 1986   Responsible Agency: FHWA

To Reach: 2.0 miles N of Fishing Bridge Jct, on W side of road in field next to a metal post, SW of pullout on E side of road.

NOTES

PID: PY0013   **Stamp: B 11 1923**   **Family: N**   **Access: N**   **Ease: M**

Coordinates: 44.59156 -110.38546   **Elevation: 7767.32**

Mon Date: 1923   **Responsible Agency: USCGS**

To Reach: 1.8 miles N of Fishing Bridge Jct, @ parking turnout, 222 ft SE of projected intersection of centerline of old road (loo for the smaller trees) and existing road, 21 ft N of old road centerline, 148 ft E of existing road centerline, in boulder projecting 1.8 ft

NOTES

PID: PY0872   **Stamp: L-19 1977**   **Family: N**   **Access: N**   **Ease: E**

Coordinates: 44.57413 -110.38293   **Elevation: 7863.18**

Mon Date: 1977   **Responsible Agency: NPS**

To Reach: 0.45 miles N of Fishing Bridge Jct, on W side of highway across from and 154 ft S of pullout, 98 ft S of dirt service road, 26 ft W of road centerline

NOTES

Yellowstone Benchmarks
East Entrance Road

From Fishing Bridge: Reset your odometer/GPS in the middle of the intersection, or as you enter the turn lane if you're coming from the south
From the East Entrance: Reset your odometer/GPS as you sit at the East Entrance Station ranger window

The benchmarks along the western third of the East Entrance Road (from Fishing Bridge to Lake Butte) are largely from the ground deformation studies conducted during the 1970s and 1980s. The eastern two thirds are from the 1923 leveling survey undertaken by the U. S. Coast and Geodetic Survey.

Many of the original 1923 markers were destroyed during the reconstruction of the road over the past twenty years. One interesting marker that remains is located atop the concrete wing wall of overpass at the old Corkscrew Bridge just east of Sylvan Pass. Getting to this marker requires a climb down a steep, rocky embankment (and back up!). Extreme care is required, so it's best to use binoculars to see it from the overlook.

PID: PY0012   Stamp: A11 1923   Family: N   Access: N   Ease: E

Coordinates: 44.5681658 -110.386202   Elevation: 7798.69

Mon Date: 1923   Responsible Agency: BPR

To Reach: 0.05 miles E of Fishing Bridge Jct, W of Fishing Bridge, 116 ft
               NW of the W point of the West Fishing Bridge pullout, in a small
               concrete monument projecting 3 ft from ground NE of the old
               roadbed

NOTES

PID: PY0874   Stamp: 84 23   Family: N   Access: N   Ease: E

Coordinates: 44.56805112 -110.3862378   Elevation: 7826.08

Mon Date: 1984   Responsible Agency: CVO

To Reach: 0.05 miles E of Fishing Bridge Jct, W of Fishing Bridge, on stone
               culvert 39 ft N of roadway centerline, 33ft S of marker PY0012

NOTES

PID: PY0876   Stamp: 31 MDC 1976   Family: N   Access: N   Ease: E

Coordinates: 44.56357 -110.37269   Elevation: 7760.86

Mon Date: 1976   Responsible Agency: USGS

To Reach: 0.85 miles E of Fishing Bridge Jct, across road from E entrance to
               YGS Dorm/Ice Kiosk Parking Lot, on westernmost manhole cover
               foundation, 25 ft S of road centerline

NOTES

PID: PY0877 Stamp: 7743.43 Family: N Access: N Ease: E

Coordinates: 44.55911 -110.35703 Elevation: 7749.78

Mon Date: 1923 Responsible Agency: BPR

To Reach: 1.6 miles E of Fishing Bridge Jct, on west abutment of bridge over Pelican Creek. Park W or E and walk to marker taking careful note of traffic.

NOTES

PID: PY0878 Stamp: CVO 84-15 Family: N Access: N Ease: E

Coordinates: 44.55795 -110.34265 Elevation: 7755.52

Mon Date: 1984 Responsible Agency: CVO

To Reach: 2.4 miles E of Fishing Bridge Jct, on S wall of stone culvert, 20 ft S of roadway, 65 ft SW of gravel pullout on N side of road.

NOTES

PID: PY0879 Stamp: 32 MDC 1976 Family: N Access: Y Ease: E

Coordinates: 44.558100 -110.33601 Elevation: 7768.01

Mon Date: 1976 Responsible Agency: USGS

To Reach: 2.75 miles E of Fishing Bridge Jct, at gravel pullout, 52 ft S of road centerline, 17 ft E of centerline of unmarked trail

NOTES

PID: PY0880 | Stamp: CVO 84 27   Family: N   Access: N   Ease: E

Coordinates: 44.5599100 -110.32297   Elevation: 7800.85

Mon Date: 1984   Responsible Agency: CVO

To Reach: 3.4 miles E of Fishing Bridge Jct, 33 ft W of easternmost pullout for Indian Pond, 20 ft S of road centerline on stone culvert head-wall

NOTES

PID: PY0881 | Stamp: CVO 84-12   Family: N   Access: N   Ease: E

Coordinates: 44.559667 -110.32291   Elevation: 7787.37

Mon Date: 1984   Responsible Agency: CVO

To Reach: 3.4 miles E of Fishing Bridge Jct, 98 ft S of road centerline, 65 ft N of the N shore of Indian Pond, in explosion debris boulder. 18 ft below level of road surface.

NOTES

PID: PY1210 | Stamp: PELICAN CO   Family: N   Access: N   Ease: D

Coordinates: 44.6481158 -110.1931215   Elevation: 9650.00

Mon Date: 1958   Responsible Agency: USGS

To Reach: 3.4 miles E of Fishing Bridge Jct, then out Pelican Creek Trail. 31 ft SE of the Pelican Cone Fire Lookout, reached via hike only. This area has heavy bear use, so take your bear spray! Full stamp reads: PELICAN CONE

NOTES

| PID: PY0882 | Stamp: CVO 84-16 | Family: N | Access: N | Ease: M |

Coordinates: 44.55453 -110.30842   **Elevation:** 7745.57

Mon Date: 1984   **Responsible Agency:** CVO

To Reach: 4.2 miles E of Fishing Bridge Jct, on NE headwall of stone culvert, 47 ft of "Mary Bay" sign, 23 ft NE of road centerline. Park in pull-out E of marker location & walk back NW for about 300 ft

NOTES

| PID: PY9912 | Stamp: CVO 93-004 | Family: N | Access: N | Ease: E |

Coordinates: 44.53218 -110.29695   **Elevation:** 7835.92

Mon Date: 1993   **Responsible Agency:** CVO

To Reach: 6.35 miles E of Fishing Bridge Jct, at Steamboat Point Picnic Area pullout, 54 ft SE of vault toilet, in bedrock, flush with ground

NOTES

| PID: PY0887 | Stamp: CVO 84 19 | Family: N | Access: Y | Ease: E |

Coordinates: 44.523600 -110.28135   **Elevation:** 7749.72

Mon Date: 1984   **Responsible Agency:** CVO

To Reach: 7.6 miles E of Fishing Bridge, on NE headwall of bridge over Sedge Creek

NOTES

PID: PY1211   Stamp: LAKE BUTTE   Family: N   Access: N   Ease: M

Coordinates: 44.51034 -110.27474   Elevation: 8353.00

Mon Date: 1950   Responsible Agency: USGS

To Reach: 9.0 miles E of Fishing Bridge Jct, then N on Lake Butte Drive
               to parking lot. 75 ft N of parking lot on trail, 20 ft higher than
               road surface. Set in pumice boulder. May be covered with dirt/
               debris. This is an azimuth station, with reference points located at
               Elk Point and Park Point across the Lake.

NOTES

PID: PY0033   Stamp: H 12 1923 8472   Family: N   Access: N   Ease: M

Coordinates: 44.50515 -110.19412   Elevation: 8477.02

Mon Date: 1923   Responsible Agency: USCGS

To Reach: 13.4 miles E of Fishing Bridge Jct at Cub Creek hairpin turn (park
               in turnout NW of hairpin). In center of boulder projecting 15"
               from ground, 541 ft N of road centerline, 94 ft W of bank of Cub
               Creek, in open field

NOTES

PID: PY0036   Stamp: K 12 1923 8413   Family: N   Access: Y   Ease: E

Coordinates: 44.478536 -110.158883   Elevation: 8418.38

Mon Date: 1923   Responsible Agency: USCGS

To Reach: 16.9 miles E of Fishing Bridge Jct, at S side of highway at Sylvan
               Lake Picnic area, in concrete pedestal

NOTES

PID: PY0037 Stamp: 8162.007 L 12   Family: N   Access: N   Ease: D

Coordinates: 44.45998 -110.11740   Elevation: 8166.85

Mon Date: 1923   Responsible Agency: USCGS

To Reach: 19.4 miles E of Fishing Bridge Jct, at abandoned Corkscrew
                 Bridge, in SE wing wall at entrance to tunnel, 5 ft S of road cen-
                 terline. Marker is very difficult to get to; requires climb down steep
                 rocky embankment

NOTES

PID: PY0041 Stamp: P 12 1923 6950   Family: N   Access: N   Ease: M

Coordinates: 44.4896667 -110.00219   Elevation: 6955.28

Mon Date: 1923   Responsible Agency: USCGS

To Reach: 0.1 miles E of East Entrance Station, at "Leaving Yellowstone"
                 sign, 147 ft N of road centerline in open space between road &
                 gov't housing area, 112 ft W/NW of the YNP sign, on monument
                 projecting 55cm above ground. Concrete pedestal was broken at
                 time of this writing.

NOTES

Yellowstone Benchmarks
Fishing Bridge to West Thumb

From Fishing Bridge: Reset your odometer/GPS in the middle of the intersection at Lake Village (not Fishing Bridge Junction)
From West Thumb: Reset your odometer/GPS in the middle of the intersection

The search for benchmarks along this stretch of roadway starts you out in Lake Village (assuming you're beginning on the north end) with the historic Lake Astro Station, the Lake Triangulation Station, and several benchmarks around the Lake Hotel. From there, you head south to find the markers at Bridge Bay and along the lake shore to West Thumb. On the way south, if you're of a mind to get off the main road for a bit, there are two markers south on the trail to Natural Bridge and continuing along the old road bed. And, if you're headed north, you can stop at the Arnica Creek/Howard Eaton turnout and head north on the old road's south end. The vintage of the markers spans the history of the surveys that have been performed in the park; the Astro marker was installed in 1893, and there are benchmarks from 1923, 1950, 1968, 1977, and 1987.

PID: PY0949   Stamp: 7738.43   Family: Y   Access: Y   Ease: E

Coordinates: 44.5546895 -110.3951003   Elevation: 7768.03

Mon Date: 1893   Responsible Agency: USCGS

To Reach: In front of Lake Lodge, 147 ft E/SE of lodge entrance, across road
                 in front of lodge, in top of 18 x 24 inch granite block. Datum is
                 simple pin in the block. Block is inscribed. Existing is reset of block
                 (PY0011) installed in 1893. This is known as the Lake Astro Sta-
                 tion.

NOTES

PID: PY0948   Stamp: YELLOWST   Family: N   Access: Y   Ease: M

Coordinates: 44.55219 -110.39352   Elevation: 7751.10

Mon Date: 1950   Responsible Agency: USCGS

To Reach: In Lake Village, 492 ft NE of N face of Lake Ranger Station, along
                 the old road bed, 16.7 ft E of road centerline, in sagebrush. Full
                 stamp reads: YELLOWSTONE 1950 7744

NOTES

PID: CQ6916   Stamp: YELLOWST   Family: N   Access: Y   Ease: M

Coordinates: 44.552162 -110.393412   Elevation: 7751.10

Mon Date: 1950   Responsible Agency: USCGS

To Reach: Reference Mark 1 for PY0948, located 20 ft ESE of PY0948.
                 May be covered by dirt and debris. Full stamp reads: YELLOW-
                 STONE RM-1

NOTES

PID: CQ6917 | Stamp: YELLOWST   Family: N   Access: Y   Ease: M

Coordinates: 44.552099 -110.393605   **Elevation: 7751.10**

Mon Date: 1950   **Responsible Agency: USCGS**

To Reach: Reference Mark 2 for PY0948, located 25 ft SW of PY0948. May be covered by dirt and debris. Full stamp reads: YELLOWSTONE RM-2

NOTES

PID: PY9918 | Stamp: L 57   Family: Y   Access: N   Ease: E

Coordinates: 44.54971 -110.39754   **Elevation: 7798.00**

Mon Date: Unknown   **Responsible Agency: Unknown**

To Reach: In Lake Village, behind old Lake YPSS Station, at top of small hill W of old station, on social trail to old gravesites. Outer ring ground away so there's no way to identify who installed it (possibly BPR)

NOTES

PID: PY0010 | Stamp: Z 10 RESET   Family: Y   Access: Y   Ease: E

Coordinates: 44.549123 -110.40109   **Elevation: 7762.51**

Mon Date: 1968   **Responsible Agency: USCGS**

To Reach: In Lake Village, across the street and 295 ft S/SW of front entrance to Lake Hotel, 59 ft S of road centerline, W of pullout in front of hotel.

NOTES

| **PID: PY0947** | Stamp: L 13 1977 | Family: Y | Access: Y | Ease: E |

Coordinates: 44.54908 -110.40044   Elevation: 7766.85

Mon Date: 1977   Responsible Agency: NPS

To Reach: In Lake Village, 288 ft S of Lake Hotel, 76 ft N of Lake shore, 10 ft S of road centerline, 5 ft S of W end of parking lot, on 1 ft white PVC pipe

NOTES

| **PID: PY9909** | Stamp: 774.63 | Family: Y | Access: Y | Ease: E |

Coordinates: 44.54939 -110.40488   Elevation: 7796.00

Mon Date: 1923   Responsible Agency: BPR

To Reach: In Lake Village, behind Fish Hatchery Bldg & behind old Lake Boathouse, 20 ft E of old road barricade, on S headwall of old bridge

NOTES

| **PID: PY0946** | Stamp: H 368 1987 | Family: N | Access: N | Ease: E |

Coordinates: 44.54573 -110.41782   Elevation: 7771.36

Mon Date: 1987   Responsible Agency: NGS

To Reach: 0.6 miles S of Lake Village Jct, 72 ft E of road centerline, 31 ft N of the NE end of large, unnamed pullout on S end of old roadbed. Logo cap

NOTES

PID: PY0945	Stamp: G 368 1987	Family: N	Access: N	Ease: M

Coordinates: 44.53857 -110.42999   **Elevation: 7779.43**

Mon Date: 1987   **Responsible Agency: NGS**

To Reach: 1.5 miles S of Lake Village Jct, on bedrock at top of road cut, 258 ft SE of the corner of a vault toilet in Bridge Bay Campground, 40 ft NW of road centerline, 10 ft above road surface level. Marker is heavily damaged

NOTES

PID: PY9913	Stamp: BB 9 1977	Family: N	Access: N	Ease: E

Coordinates: 44.53857 -110.42966   **Elevation: 7799.00**

Mon Date: 1977   **Responsible Agency: NPS**

To Reach: 1.5 miles S of Lake Village Jct, 20 ft N of the N end of paved pull-out on E side of road, across the road from PY0945, level with road surface, right in front of red metal post

NOTES

PID: PY0943	Stamp: 2 MDC 1977	Family: N	Access: N	Ease: E

Coordinates: 44.53176 -110.4353   **Elevation: 7761.43**

Mon Date: 1977   **Responsible Agency: USGS**

To Reach: 2.05 miles S of Lake Village Jct, on S end of W side of Bridge Bay bridge.

NOTES

PID: PY0007   Stamp: W 10 1923   Family: N   Access: N   Ease: D

Coordinates: 44.5244 -110.45893   Elevation: 7849.95

Mon Date: 1923   Responsible Agency: USCGS

To Reach: 2.1 miles S of Lake Village Jct, then 1.2 miles S on old service road
                 (trail), on W side of road in road cut, 6x10 ft lava outcrop, 10.5 ft
                 W of road centerline, 3 ft above road surface level

NOTES

PID: PY0941   Stamp: PIT 1987   Family: N   Access: N   Ease: D

Coordinates: 44.52004 -110.47298   Elevation: 8035.98

Mon Date: 1987   Responsible Agency: NGS

To Reach: 2.1 miles S of Lake Village Jct, then 2 miles S on old service road,
                 near center of SE edge of remediated gravel pit, 111 ft NW of dirt
                 road centerline, 7 meters above road level. Requires 2-mile hike.
                 Logo cap

NOTES

PID: PY0935   Stamp: A 368 1987   Family: N   Access: N   Ease: M

Coordinates: 44.48881 -110.53276   Elevation: 7963.63

Mon Date: 1987   Responsible Agency: NGS

To Reach: 5.8 miles N of West Thumb Jct, then 1.0 miles N on old highway, 5
                 ft NE of utility pole #145. Requires 1-mile hike. Logo cap

NOTES

PID: PY0934   Stamp: 6 MDC 1977   Family: N   Access: N   Ease: E

Coordinates: 44.47743 -110.54359   Elevation: 7774.68

Mon Date: 1977   Responsible Agency: USGS

To Reach: 5.8 miles N of West Thumb Jct, 67 ft NW of road centerline, across
from large pullout, 4.5 ft NE of N end of barricade fence, encased
in white PVC pipe.

NOTES

PID: PY0933   Stamp: 7 MDC 1977   Family: N   Access: N   Ease: E

Coordinates: 44.451091 -110.563738   Elevation: 7839.27

Mon Date: 1977   Responsible Agency: USGS

To Reach: 3.4 miles N of West Thumb Jct, on N end of headwall on E side of
road, 19 ft E of road centerline.

NOTES

PID: PY0931   Stamp: WT 2 1977   Family: N   Access: N   Ease: M

Coordinates: 44.4232627 -110.5752   Elevation: 7768.60

Mon Date: 1977   Responsible Agency: NPS

To Reach: 0.7 miles N of West Thumb Jct, W of long pullout @ Occasional
Geyser (no sign), 40 ft W of road centerline, 1.6 from metal post, 3
ft above road surface level.

NOTES

PID: PY9911   Stamp: WT 4 1977   Family: N   Access: N   Ease: D

Coordinates: 44.41498 -110.57062   **Elevation:** 7817.00

Mon Date: 1977   **Responsible Agency:** NPS

To Reach: 0.1 miles N of West Thumb Jct, in West Thumb Geyser Basin, 600
ft SE down abandoned road to the S (not the SE road), in wooded
area W of field, 175 ft N of old sewer pumping station building,
next to metal pole

NOTES

Yellowstone Benchmarks
South Entrance Road

From South Entrance Station: Reset your odometer/GPS as you sit at the South Entrance Station ranger window

From West Thumb: Reset your odometer/GPS in the middle of the West Thumb Junction (you'll need to reset it to zero again at the Grant Village Intersection as well)

The markers for this stretch of road begin behind the Snake River Ranger Station at the South Entrance. There are two located on the bridge over the Lewis River at Lewis Falls, as well as an undocumented one from a 1930 installation by the Bureau of Public Roads, located adjacent to the walkway up to the little overlook on the south side of the river where you can see the falls. On the north end, one of the benchmarks requires a half-mile hike back to the old Grant Village Incinerator site. Private vehicles are not allowed on this road (even if the gate is open).

| PID: PY0071 | Stamp: S 13 | Family: N | Access: Y | Ease: E |

Coordinates: 44.13608 -110.66618   Elevation: 6930.64

Mon Date: 1923   Responsible Agency: USCGS

To Reach: At South Entrance Station, behind Snake River Ranger Station Bldg, 25 ft E of SE corner of bldg on exposed boulder flush with the ground (stamp may appear to some as S 15)

NOTES

| PID: PY9914 | Stamp: 14-2 1986 | Family: N | Access: Y | Ease: E |

Coordinates: 44.13689 -110.66608   Elevation: 7032.30

Mon Date: 1986   Responsible Agency: FHWA

To Reach: 0.15 miles N of South Ent Sta, turn E into Snake River Picnic Area, 300 ft E of road centerline, near E edge of Picnic Area, 13 ft E of centerline of easternmost road in Picnic Area, 65ft W of bank of river

NOTES

| PID: PY0828 | Stamp: 13 MDC 1977 | Family: N | Access: N | Ease: E |

Coordinates: 44.15149 -110.67316   Elevation: 7002.49

Mon Date: 1977   Responsible Agency: USGS

To Reach: 1.15 miles N of South Ent Sta, on south end of west wall of bridge over Crawfish Creek

NOTES

| PID: PY0827 | Stamp: Q 369 1987 | Family: N | Access: N | Ease: M |

Coordinates: 44.15181 -110.673240   Elevation: 6989.51

Mon Date: 1987   Responsible Agency: NGS

To Reach: 1.15 miles N of South Entrance Station, on NE bank of Crawfish Creek below the bridge, 47 ft NE of road centerline, 10 ft below road level. Park in large pullout on NE side of bridge, take first dirt trail down toward river (marker is between bridge and brink of falls)

NOTES

| PID: PY0826 | Stamp: P 369 1987 | Family: N | Access: N | Ease: M |

Coordinates: 44.15833 -110.67155   Elevation: 7124.92

Mon Date: 1987   Responsible Agency: NGS

To Reach: 1.7 miles N of South Entrance Station, at S end of overgrown gravel pullout (hard to spot) for old service road, 43 ft E of road centerline, 15 ft E/NE of centerline of old roadbed. Logo cap

NOTES

| PID: PY0825 | Stamp: 12 MDC 1977 | Family: N | Access: N | Ease: E |

Coordinates: 44.16471 -110.66666   Elevation: 7235.37

Mon Date: 1977   Responsible Agency: USGS

To Reach: 2.25 miles N of South Ent Sta, across road from center of gravel pullout at exit from old roadbed, 20 ft E of road centerline, on a 1x3 boulder projecting 1 ft from ground

NOTES

PID: PY0821	Stamp: H 369 1987	Family: N	Access: N	Ease: M

Coordinates: 44.19834 -110.6586   Elevation: 7720.51

Mon Date: 1987   Responsible Agency: NGS

To Reach: 4.7 miles N of South Entrance Sta, SW end of 3x10 exposed bed-
              rock, @ S end of road cut, 23 ft E of road centerline, 9 ft N of N
              end of guardrail. Park in pullout S of guardrail's S end and walk N
              to other end

NOTES

PID: PY0816	Stamp: 50 RDS 1955	Family: N	Access: N	Ease: D

Coordinates: 44.24374 -110.64794   Elevation: 7756.43

Mon Date: 1955   Responsible Agency: USGS

To Reach: 8.25 miles N of South Entrance Station, park at Pitchstone Plateau
              Trailhead, take trail until it turns N, then 32 ft up trail, then 33 ft
              east off trail to marker & sign on felled tree

NOTES

PID: PY0814	Stamp: 14-4 1986	Family: Y	Access: N	Ease: E

Coordinates: 44.2674681 -110.6345781   Elevation: 7727.19

Mon Date: 1986   Responsible Agency: FHWA

To Reach: 9.5 miles S of Grant Village Jct, on SE corner of walkway of bridge
              over Lewis River at Lewis Falls. Near marker PY0813

NOTES

PID: PY0813   Stamp: LEWIS FALLS   Family: Y   Access: N   Ease: E

Coordinates: 44.26744 -110.6347   Elevation: 7694.88

Mon Date: 1987   Responsible Agency: NGS

To Reach: 9.5 miles S of Grant Village Jct, near SE corner of walkway on bridge over Lewis River at Lewis Falls. 14 ft N of marker 14-4

NOTES

PID: PY9924   Stamp: 555 + 799   Family: Y   Access: N   Ease: E

Coordinates: 44.267564, -110.635050   Elevation: 7702.58

Mon Date: 1930   Responsible Agency: BPR

To Reach: 9.45 miles S of Grant Village Jct, park at Lewis Falls parking area and walk up dirt trail to falls overlook. Marker is on block at ground level mounted in concrete with "RD PT" carved in it.

NOTES

PID: PY0812   Stamp: C 369 1987   Family: N   Access: N   Ease: M

Coordinates: 44.2681 -110.63358   Elevation: 7731.72

Mon Date: 1987   Responsible Agency: NGS

To Reach: 9.45 miles S of Grant Village Jct, in exposed bedrock at road cut, 59 ft NE of the N corner of bridge over Lewis River, 28 ft NW of road centerline, 3 ft above road level

NOTES

| **PID: PY0066** | **Stamp:** M13 1923 | **Family:** N | **Access:** N | **Ease:** E |

Coordinates: 44.28287 -110.62644   **Elevation:** 7811.07

Mon Date: 1923   **Responsible Agency:** USCGS

To Reach: 8.3 miles S of Grant Village Jct, 40 ft S of road centerline, S of Lewis Lake Campground Entrance Rd, on top of large boulder in the trees

| NOTES |

| **PID: PY0810** | **Stamp:** B 369 1987 | **Family:** N | **Access:** N | **Ease:** M |

Coordinates: 44.28309 -110.62627   **Elevation:** 7812.49

Mon Date: 1987   **Responsible Agency:** NGS

To Reach: 8.3 miles S of Grant Village Jct, in exposed bedrock, across from entrance road into Lewis Lake Campground, 65 ft NW of Lewis Lake Campground sign, 19 ft NE of road centerline (E side of road). May be covered by dirt/debris

| NOTES |

| **PID: PY0809** | **Stamp:** 10 MDC 1977 | **Family:** N | **Access:** N | **Ease:** E |

Coordinates: 44.29377 -110.614359   **Elevation:** 7798.05

Mon Date: 1977   **Responsible Agency:** USGS

To Reach: 7.2 miles S of Grant Village Rd, on culvert headwall on E side of road, 18 ft N of gravel pullout on west side of roadway

| NOTES |

PID: PY0808	Stamp: A 369 1987	Family: N	Access: N	Ease: M

Coordinates: 44.29515 -110.61358   Elevation: 7793.08

Mon Date: 1987   Responsible Agency: NGS

To Reach: 7.1 miles S of Grant Village Jct, on exposed bedrock across from pullout, 17 ft E of road centerline, 3 ft SE of SE corner of storm drain. May be covered by dirt/debris

NOTES

PID: PY0807	Stamp: 86-11	Family: N	Access: N	Ease: M

Coordinates: 44.30899 -110.60231   Elevation: 7788.67

Mon Date: 1986   Responsible Agency: CVO

To Reach: 6.0 miles S of Grant Village Jct, on E headwall of stone culvert, 65 ft SE of long, narrow pullout on west side of road, 19 ft E of road centerline

NOTES

PID: PY1238	Stamp: SHERIDAN	Family: N	Access: N	Ease: D

Coordinates: 44.2662195 -110.5292859   Elevation: 10313.00

Mon Date: 1950   Responsible Agency: USCGS

To Reach: At summit of Mt. Sheridan near fire lookout

NOTES

PID: PY0806   Stamp: 19   Family: N   Access: N   Ease: M

Coordinates: 44.31920 -110.59859   Elevation: 7794.88

Mon Date: 1923   Responsible Agency: BPR

To Reach: 5.25 miles S of Grant Village Jct, on E headwall of stone culvert, 20 ft E of road centerline, approx 300 ft S of Lewis Channel/Dogshead Trailhead Pullout

NOTES

PID: PY1129   Stamp: CVO86-14   Family: N   Access: N   Ease: M

Coordinates: 44.35681 -110.58302   Elevation: 7984.10

Mon Date: 1986   Responsible Agency: CVO

To Reach: 2.45 miles S of Grant Village Jct, 0.1 miles S of Riddle Lake Trailhead, on stone culvert on W side of road.

NOTES

PID: PY1131   Stamp: CVO86-16   Family: N   Access: N   Ease: E

Coordinates: 44.38034 -110.57533   Elevation: 7943.42

Mon Date: 1986   Responsible Agency: CVO

To Reach: 0.75 miles S of Grant Village Jct, on stone culvert W and 5 ft below highway, just S of small gravel pullout

NOTES

PID: PY1132	Stamp: NPS GV2 1977	Family: N	Access: N	Ease: E

Coordinates: 44.39096 -110.57192   Elevation: 7854.97

Mon Date: 1977   Responsible Agency: NPS

To Reach: 1.7 miles S of West Thumb Jct, @ Grant Village Jct, W of intersection, 5 meters NW of directional information sign intended for those exiting Grant Village. Surrounded by white PVC pipe

NOTES

PID: PY0805	Stamp: GS 1 1977	Family: N	Access: N	Ease: M

Coordinates: 44.39535 -110.57523   Elevation: 7838.35

Mon Date: 1977   Responsible Agency: NPS

To Reach: 1.25 miles S of West Thumb Jct, 0.35 miles W on Grant Village Incinerator Service Rd (hike only; no private vehicles allowed), on N retaining wall of old incinerator pad. NPS marker, may be missing, incinerator was removed in 2010

NOTES

PID: PY0804	Stamp: BIGTHUMB	Family: N	Access: Y	Ease: E

Coordinates: 44.40498 -110.56919   Elevation: 7763.76

Mon Date: 1987   Responsible Agency: NGS

To Reach: 0.8 miles S of West Thumb Jct, in SE corner of walkway on bridge over Big Thumb Creek.

NOTES

| PID: PY0803 | Stamp: 9 MDC 1977 | Family: N | Access: Y | Ease: E |

Coordinates: 44.40549 -110.5695451   **Elevation:** 7792.03

Mon Date: 1977   **Responsible Agency:** USGS

To Reach: 0.75 miles S of West Thumb Jct, on top of NW guardrail of bridge over Big Thumb Creek

NOTES

Yellowstone Benchmarks
West Thumb to Old Faithful

From West Thumb: Reset your odometer/GPS in the middle of the intersection

From Old Faithful: Reset your odometer/GPS under the Old Faithful overpass as you head south

The majority of the benchmarks found along this stretch of road are from the 1976 USGS, 1986 FHWA, or 1987 NGS surveys. There are a couple of interesting markers remaining from the 1923 USCGS surveys, however. The F-10 marker at Kepler Cascades has been damaged, as has the K-10 marker at Isa Lake; only the pedestals remain. Their brother, L-10, a few miles down the road at Herron Creek, remains intact. Most of the other "10" markers from the 1923 leveling surveys are located along the old roadbed some distance to the north.

There are three markers on the bridge over the Firehole River south of the main Old Faithful Interchange. This is known as the "Bear's Playground" area because the bears used to congregate at the small, often seasonal lake in the woods just to the west of the bridge as they awaited being fed garbage at the nearby Old Faithful Auto Campground (in the 1920s/30s). The lake itself is known as "Bear's Playground," in fact. You'll note a pair of benchmarks labeled "MEERTENS" on the easternmost end of the bridge. The original marker was installed on the "floating" part of the bridge inside the expansion joint. Since this portion of the bridge moves (even if ever so slightly), and this is a horizontal control point, the original marker was deemed unstable for its intended purpose and thus, MEERTENS 2 was installed outside the expansion joint. The #2 marker is therefore the "official" benchmark for this station.

PID: PY9910 Stamp: POT   Family: N   Access: N   Ease: M

Coordinates: 44.41393 -110.57874   Elevation: 7809.00

Mon Date: Unknown   Responsible Agency: BPR

To Reach: At West Thumb Jct, 18 ft SW of (behind) direction/distance sign, on concrete flush with ground. May be covered by grass/dirt and hard to see. Marker 54 MDC 1976 (PY0801) was supposed to be 1 meter SE of this, but is apparently covered by downed trees.

NOTES

PID: PY0800 Stamp: T 367 1987   Family: N   Access: N   Ease: E

Coordinates: 44.41882 -110.5847499   Elevation: 7903.10

Mon Date: 1987   Responsible Agency: NGS

To Reach: 0.45 miles W of West Thumb Jct, 68 ft NE of road centerline, 53 ft NE of pipe barricade, 25 ft SE of the S corner of an abandoned 9x10 concrete pad, level with road surface. Logo cap

NOTES

PID: PY0798 Stamp: 53 MDC 1976   Family: N   Access: N   Ease: E

Coordinates: 44.42134 -110.59218   Elevation: 8084.55

Mon Date: 1976   Responsible Agency: USGS

To Reach: 1.1 miles W of West Thumb Jct, on E headwall of stone culvert, 36 ft S of old roadbed centerline, 22 ft W of main road centerline

NOTES

PID: PY0799	Stamp: S 367 1987	Family: N	Access: N	Ease: E

Coordinates: 44.421590 -110.59246 — Elevation: 8095.85

Mon Date: 1987 — Responsible Agency: NGS

To Reach: 1.1 miles W of West Thumb Jct, 87 ft W of road centerline, 34 ft N of the center of old roadbed, at top of small hill. Logo cap.

NOTES

PID: PY1135	Stamp: 1986T 10-34	Family: N	Access: N	Ease: E

Coordinates: 44.43354 -110.6436 — Elevation: 8448.00

Mon Date: 1986 — Responsible Agency: FHWA

To Reach: 4.3 miles W of West Thumb Jct, just west of easternmost Continental Divide pullout, 125 ft S of road centerline in large clearing, right next to a metal post. Area may be waterlogged/marshy

NOTES

PID: PY1278	Stamp: SHOSHONE	Family: N	Access: N	Ease: E

Coordinates: 44.43357 -110.64363 — Elevation: 8449.28

Mon Date: 1987 — Responsible Agency: NGS

To Reach: 4.3 miles W of West Thumb Jct, just west of easternmost Continental Divide pullout, 100 ft S of road centerline in a large clearing. 21ft NNE of PY1135. Logo cap. Area may be waterlogged/marshy

NOTES

PID: PY0793 | Stamp: N 367 1987   Family: N   Access: N   Ease: M

Coordinates: 44.44746 -110.69822   Elevation: 7985.07

Mon Date: 1987   Responsible Agency: NGS

To Reach: 8.55 miles W of West Thumb Jct, Delacy Picnic Area, 52 ft NW of road centerline, 32 ft N of SW entrance to Picnic Area, in wooded area. Logo cap

NOTES

PID: PY0055 | Stamp: L 10 RESET   Family: N   Access: N   Ease: M

Coordinates: 44.44801 -110.70743   Elevation: 8021.83

Mon Date: 1937   Responsible Agency: USCGS

To Reach: 9.0 miles W of West Thumb Jct, on E bank of Herron Creek (no sign), 24 ft N of road centerline, in concrete post

NOTES

PID: PY0053 | Stamp: K 10 RESET   Family: Y   Access: N   Ease: E

Coordinates: 44.44217 -110.71808   Elevation: 8268.09

Mon Date: 1936   Responsible Agency: USCGS

To Reach: 9.8 miles W of West Thumb Jct, @ Continental Divide/Isa Lake pullout, 5 ft E of E end of Isa Lake, marker is missing, but damaged concrete pedestal remains. The L 367 (PY0791) benchmark is supposed to be a few feet from this, but was not found by press time.

NOTES

PID: PY0789 Stamp: 51 MDC 1976   Family: N   Access: N   Ease: D

Coordinates: 44.43467 -110.73476   Elevation: 8066.65

Mon Date: 1976   Responsible Agency: USGS

To Reach: 10.85 miles W of West Thumb Jct, 59 ft SW of Divide Lookout
              Trailhead sign, on a small hill, encased in green PVC pipe. May be
              covered with dirt/debris

NOTES

PID: PY0788 Stamp: J 367 1987   Family: N   Access: N   Ease: E

Coordinates: 44.43175 -110.74787   Elevation: 7982.36

Mon Date: 1987   Responsible Agency: NGS

To Reach: 11.6 miles W of West Thumb Jct, @ SW end of pullout, 68 ft NW
              of road centerline, 8 ft above road surface on top of boulder with
              dead trees lying on it

NOTES

PID: PY0784 Stamp: G 367 1987   Family: N   Access: N   Ease: M

Coordinates: 44.43756 -110.79857   Elevation: 7757.75

Mon Date: 1987   Responsible Agency: NGS

To Reach: 14.4 miles W of West Thumb Jct, 0.7 miles south of entrance to
              Lone Star Trailhead, NW of highway pullout, NE end of rock
              ledge, 99 ft NE of the road centerline, 7.5 ft SE of wash leading
              to storm drain

NOTES

| PID: PY0048 | Stamp: F 10 1923 7583 | Family: Y | Access: Y | Ease: E |

Coordinates: 44.44614 -110.80592   **Elevation:** 7589.74

Mon Date: 1923   **Responsible Agency:** BPR

To Reach: 2.4 miles S of Old Faithful Interchange, at Kepler Cascade, immediately next to walkway at its entrance, on left-hand side. Monument remains, but benchmark is missing

NOTES

| PID: PY0781 | Stamp: A 1976 | Family: N | Access: N | Ease: E |

Coordinates: 44.45415 -110.81918   **Elevation:** 7400.84

Mon Date: 1976   **Responsible Agency:** NPS

To Reach: 1.5 miles S of Old Faithful Interchange, on E corner of the N walkway on the Firehole River Bridge @ Bear's Playground

NOTES

| PID: PY0779 | Stamp: MEERTENS | Family: N | Access: N | Ease: E |

Coordinates: 44.45404 -110.81915   **Elevation:** 7399.60

Mon Date: 1987   **Responsible Agency:** NGS

To Reach: 1.5 miles S of Old Faithful Interchange, 2 markers (3 feet apart) @ E corner of the south side of the walkway on the Firehole Bridge at Bear's Playground. MEERTENS (PY0779) was deemed unstable, so replacement marker MEERTENS 2 (PY0802) was installed.

NOTES

PID: PY0780   Stamp: Y 366 1987   Family: N   Access: Y   Ease: E

Coordinates: 44.45556 -110.83421   Elevation: 7364.93

Mon Date: 1987   Responsible Agency: NGS

To Reach: 0.7 miles S of Old Faithful Interchange, at crosswalk, 37 feet southeast of old Haynes Finishing Shop Storage Bldg, 32 ft W of the employee pedestrian crossing/fire road from the Old Faithful Government Area

NOTES

PID: PY1142   Stamp: 10-1   Family: N   Access: N   Ease: M

Coordinates: 44.4593 -110.84079   Elevation: 7344.70

Mon Date: 1986   Responsible Agency: FHWA

To Reach: 0.1 miles SE of Old Faithful Interchange, in woods 150 ft SW of Old Faithful Access Rd centerline; located in concrete monument in clearing flush with ground, SE of "Two-Way Traffic" sign for S/B traffic. NGS datasheet indicates there's a metal fence post 3 ft away, but post is missing. May be covered with dirt/debris.

NOTES

PID: PY0778   Stamp: 10-2 1986   Family: N   Access: N   Ease: E

Coordinates: 44.46091 -110.84504   Elevation: 7345.68

Mon Date: 1986   Responsible Agency: FHWA

To Reach: 7 feet south of the southeastern end of the Old Faithful Interchange overpass bridge. Stop on main road & climb up hill.

NOTES

| PID: PY0777 | Stamp: OF-4 76 | Family: N   Access: N   Ease: E |

Coordinates: 44.46092 -110.84505   **Elevation:** 7346.49

Mon Date: 1976   **Responsible Agency:** NPS

To Reach: On southeastern end of Old Faithful Interchange overpass bridge under the guardrail. Stop on main road under overpass and climb up hill. Do NOT stop on the bridge or the approach ramps.

| NOTES |

Yellowstone Benchmarks
Old Faithful to Madison Junction

From Old Faithful: Reset your odometer/GPS under the Old Faithful overpass as you head north
From Madison Junction: Reset your odometer/GPS in the middle of the intersection

Begin your search for benchmarks in this area in front of the Old Faithful Lodge (not the Snow Lodge), between the parking area for the Lobby and the Warming Yurts. An old, undocumented BPR benchmark can be found in the woods there (the original road through the Old Faithful area ran right past this marker until 1972). Then proceed north where you'll find many of the original 1923 markers, along with several installed during the 1976 USGS and 1987 NGS surveys. See the historical section for information about the marker that used to be located in front of Old Faithful herself.

There is a benchmark approximately 20 feet north of the bridge at the Fairy Falls Trailhead (stamped "THERMAL"). This marker is often hard to see, especially during the high runoff periods in the spring. The marker is becoming encrusted from sediments in the runoff channels from Rabbit Creek and will eventually become completely unreadable

PID: PY9903   Stamp: 312.46   Family: Y   Access: Y   Ease: E

Coordinates: 44.4585997 -110.82646   Elevation: 7362

Mon Date: 1923   Responsible Agency: BPR

To Reach: In wooded area SW of Old Faithful Lodge, 65 ft N of N section of E parking lot, 50 ft ENE of the winter Warming Yurts.

NOTES

PID: PY0776   Stamp: 48 MDC 1976   Family: N   Access: N   Ease: E

Coordinates: 44.49038 -110.84763   Elevation: 7295.98

Mon Date: 1976   Responsible Agency: USGS

To Reach: 0.8 miles north of OF Interchange, 67 feet SE of the SE corner of the pullout in concrete recessed into the ground

NOTES

PID: PY0775   Stamp: 7273.15   Family: N   Access: Y   Ease: E

Coordinates: 44.4828602 -110.85258   Elevation: 7279.04

Mon Date: 1923   Responsible Agency: BPR

To Reach: 1.8 miles N of OF Interchange, near Biscuit Basin, SW end of the West walkway of the Firehole River Bridge

NOTES

PID: PY0045   Stamp: D10 1923 7337   Family: N   Access: N   Ease: M

Coordinates: 44.4798900 -110.84902   Elevation: 7343.80

Mon Date: 1923   Responsible Agency: USCGS

To Reach: 1.9 miles N of OF Interchange, E then SE on trail to Artemisia Geyser, 110 ft NE of Gem Pool, & 20 ft W of the old roadbed/trail in the tree line N of Gem Pool, on concrete post. Total of 0.37 mile hike from trailhead.

NOTES

PID: PY9920   Stamp: OF-5 1976   Family: N   Access: N   Ease: D

Coordinates: 44.4870500 -110.86599   Elevation: 7802.00

Mon Date: 1976   Responsible Agency: NPS

To Reach: 2.0 miles N of Old Faithful Interchange. Park in the Biscuit Basin Parking Lot and hike to the Observation Point above Mystic Falls (2.3 mile hike if you go via Mystic Falls)

NOTES

PID: PY0774   Stamp: X 366 1987   Family: N   Access: N   Ease: E

Coordinates: 44.490161 -110.848072   Elevation: 7286.40

Mon Date: 1987   Responsible Agency: NGS

To Reach: 2.4 miles N of Old Faithful Interchange, 60.7 Ft S of the SE corner of pullout.

NOTES

PID: PY0771 **Stamp: THERMAL** **Family: N** **Access: N** **Ease: E**

Coordinates: 44.5160979 -110.8326355 **Elevation: 7209.44**

Mon Date: 1987 **Responsible Agency: NGS**

To Reach: 4.3 miles N of Old Faithful Interchange, in exposed bedrock on shore of Firehole River approx 20 ft N of bridge @ Fairy Falls Trailhead. May be in thermal spring or creek channel. Mark unreadable

NOTES

PID: PY0148 **Stamp: C10 1923 7237** **Family: Y** **Access: Y** **Ease: E**

Coordinates: 44.5160100 -110.832760 **Elevation: 7243.14**

Mon Date: 1923 **Responsible Agency: USCGS**

To Reach: 4.3 miles N of Old Faithful Interchange, on the SE abutment of the old iron bridge across the Firehole River at the Fairy Falls Trailhead.

NOTES

PID: PY1264 **Stamp: 1956 MIDWAY** **Family: N** **Access: N** **Ease: D**

Coordinates: 44.5263100 -110.83269 **Elevation: 7255.00**

Mon Date: 1955 **Responsible Agency: USGS**

To Reach: 5.6 miles N of OF Interchange, on top of rock protruding out from Midway Bluff, across the road from Midway Geyser Basin. Requires hike up steep unmaintained social trail. Note that the NGS datasheet contains errors regarding this benchmark (refers to a no-longer present benchmark w/ same name along the old boardwalk)

NOTES

PID: PY0763   Stamp: U 366 1987   Family: N   Access: N   Ease: M

Coordinates: 44.534350 -110.81917   Elevation: 7156.07

Mon Date: 1987   Responsible Agency: NGS

To Reach: 6.7 miles N of Old Faithful Interchange, SW of intersection with Firehole Lake Drive, on bedrock outcropping, 65 ft E of the N end of a pipe culvert, 36 ft E of the road centerline, 10ft+ above road. Note: NGS datasheet geolocation is several miles off from actual

NOTES

PID: PY0769   Stamp: 45 MDC 1976   Family: N   Access: N   Ease: E

Coordinates: 44.532670 -110.8274   Elevation: 7249.16

Mon Date: 1976   Responsible Agency: USGS

To Reach: 9.4 miles S of Madison Jct, S of intersection at Whiskey Flats Picnic Area, 40 ft SE of main road centerline, and 40 ft SW of centerline of Picnic Area road. Encased in green PVC pipe. May be marshy or covered w/ debris

NOTES

PID: PY0767   Stamp: 43 MDC 1976   Family: N   Access: N   Ease: M

Coordinates: 44.5551900 -110.8074   Elevation: 7260.39

Mon Date: 1976   Responsible Agency: USGS

To Reach: 7.6 miles S of Madison Jct, in a 2 x 8 rock outcropping, on S side of small highway cut, 43 ft N of stone culvert, 39 ft E of road centerline

NOTES

PID: PY0765   Stamp: NEZ PERCE   Family: N   Access: N   Ease: E

Coordinates: 44.5731658 -110.8200073   Elevation: 7182.38

Mon Date: 1987   Responsible Agency: NGS

To Reach: 6.1 miles S of Madison Jct, 185 ft E of the NE corner of the bridge over the Nez Perce Creek, 37 ft N of creek bank.

NOTES

PID: PY0764   Stamp: 42 MDC 1976   Family: N   Access: N   Ease: E

Coordinates: 44.584623 -110.82989   Elevation: 7168.65

Mon Date: 1976   Responsible Agency: USGS

To Reach: 5.1 miles S of Madison Jct, in N end of pullout on W side of road, near the top of a 3ft domed boulder, 58 ft W of road centerline

NOTES

PID: PY0146   Stamp: Z 9 1923 7153   Family: N   Access: Y   Ease: E

Coordinates: 44.5981200 -110.83125   Elevation: 7159.11

Mon Date: 1923   Responsible Agency: USCGS

To Reach: 4.15 miles S of Madison Jct, 31 ft NE of road centerline on a 1-ft concrete post, 144 ft SW of Firehole Gravel Pit Service Road barricade, 25 ft E of road centerline, alongside roadway

NOTES

PID: PY0762   **Stamp: 41 MDC 1976**   **Family: N**   **Access: N**   **Ease: E**

Coordinates: 44.6072560 -110.84608   **Elevation: 7134.91**

Mon Date: 1976   **Responsible Agency: USGS**

To Reach: 3.3 miles S of Madison Jct in a pullout on W side of the road. Monument set in top of 10 x 20 boulder, 31 ft SW of road centerline

NOTES

PID: PY0145   **Stamp: Y 9 1923 7103**   **Family: Y**   **Access: Y**   **Ease: E**

Coordinates: 44.6171500 -110.85562   **Elevation: 7108.58**

Mon Date: 1923   **Responsible Agency: USCGS**

To Reach: 1.95 miles S of Madison Jct on Firehole Canyon Rd, SW of the bend just before junction with main road, 200 ft N of upper Firehole Cascade.

NOTES

PID: PY0709   **Stamp: 40 MDC 1976**   **Family: N**   **Access: N**   **Ease: M**

Coordinates: 44.62988 -110.85587   **Elevation: 7036.06**

Mon Date: 1976   **Responsible Agency: USGS**

To Reach: 1.35 miles S of Madison Jct, 54 ft N of the NE end of paved pullout, on an 8x10 exposed bedrock across ditch 10ft above road surface, 67 ft W of road centerline. Use care climbing rocks.

NOTES

| PID: PY0708 | Stamp: E 339 1983 | Family: N | Access: N | Ease: M |

Coordinates: 44.635326 -110.858515   **Elevation:** 6953.91

Mon Date: 1983   **Responsible Agency:** NGS

To Reach: 0.85 miles S of Madison Jct, 122 ft S of Madison Water Tank Service Rd in center (crease) of 3x3 rock 1.5 ft above the road level, 27 feet W of highway centerline. May be covered by dirt

NOTES

Yellowstone Benchmarks
West Entrance Road

From West Entrance: Reset your odometer/GPS as you pass in front of the West Yellowstone Museum headed east

From Madison Junction: Reset your odometer/GPS in the middle of the intersection

The benchmarks along this stretch of roadway are almost all from the 1923, 1960, and 1987 surveys; the 1960 surveys were conducted in the aftermath of the Hebgen Lake Earthquake in 1959. Note that as you travel eastward looking for the markers, you'll need to take the old Riverside Road scenic bypass. There are no markers along the main road in this area.

| **PID: PY0352** | Stamp: C 144 1959 | Family: N | Access: N | Ease: E |

Coordinates: 44.65563 -111.08068   Elevation: 6684.75

Mon Date: 1959   Responsible Agency: USCGS

To Reach: 1.05 mile E of West Yellowstone Museum, 0.55 miles E of W.E. Sta, NE of intersection w/ Barns Hole Road (first gravel road on your left as you head east), 58 ft N of road centerline, metal post next to it. Watch out for the huge ant hill next to the marker!!!

NOTES

| **PID: PY0950** | Stamp: WE-2 1986 | Family: N | Access: N | Ease: M |

Coordinates: 44.65368687 -111.0700652   Elevation: 6691.97

Mon Date: 1986   Responsible Agency: FHWA

To Reach: 1.55 miles E of West Yellowstone Museum, 25 ft N of road centerline, 3 ft from witness post. May be buried by dirt/debris; no pullout, but there is sufficient shoulder to pull off.

NOTES

| **PID: PY0713** | Stamp: D 566 1983 | Family: N | Access: N | Ease: M |

Coordinates: 44.65201 -111.06096   Elevation: 6695.98

Mon Date: 1983   Responsible Agency: NGS

To Reach: 2.1 miles E of West Yellowstone Museum, 0.05 miles E of unnamed fishing road, 49 ft S of road centerline, 28 ft E of old track road (barely visible) leading S, 25 ft S of flashing bison warning sign, Logo cap

NOTES

PID: PY0354   Stamp: E 130 1959   Family: N   Access: N   Ease: M

Coordinates: 44.65257 -111.04314   Elevation: 6702.36

Mon Date: 1959   Responsible Agency: USCGS

To Reach: 3.0 miles E of West Yellowstone Museum, 0.1 miles W of W turn-out for Two Ribbons Trail, 0.15 mile E of curve, 133 ft S of road centerline, in top of a large rock in treed area, 2 ft above ground level

NOTES

PID: PY0712   Stamp: B 339 1983   Family: N   Access: N   Ease: E

Coordinates: 44.65236175 -111.0392733   Elevation: 6697.58

Mon Date: 1983   Responsible Agency: NGS

To Reach: 3.2 miles E of West Yellowstone Museum, 53 ft W of W turnout road into Two Ribbons Trailhead, 51 ft N of centerline of main road, 23 ft NE of 24" pipe, Logo cap

NOTES

PID: PY0355   Stamp: C 14 1923 6706   Family: N   Access: N   Ease: M

Coordinates: 44.65015382 -111.020885   Elevation: 6711.75

Mon Date: 1923   Responsible Agency: USCGS

To Reach: 4.15 miles E of West Yellowstone Museum, 28 ft N of road centerline, in top of round rock projecting 1 ft. 0.15 miles W of curve

NOTES

PID: PY0711 | Stamp: C 339 1983   Family: N   Access: N   Ease: E

Coordinates: 44.6496233 -111.0179541   Elevation: 6720.51

Mon Date: 1983   Responsible Agency: NGS

To Reach: 4.3 miles E of West Yellowstone Museum, 63 ft S of road center-line, & 27 ft S of centerline of track road (old stagecoach road), E/SE of boulders that close road from traffic. Logo cap. Marker surrounded by trees/downed trees

NOTES

PID: PY0356 | Stamp: V 158 1960   Family: N   Access: N   Ease: D

Coordinates: 44.65102 -111.00175   Elevation: 6751.39

Mon Date: 1960   Responsible Agency: USCGS

To Reach: 5.1 miles E of West Yellowstone Museum, inside strip of land between main road and Riverside Drive, 55 ft N of main road centerline, 33 ft E of centerline of curve in Riverside, SW of speed limit sign in woods, in concrete. May be covered by dirt/debris and fallen trees.

NOTES

PID: PY0077 | Stamp: B 14 1923 6735   Family: N   Access: N   Ease: E

Coordinates: 44.6603194 -110.9912525   Elevation: 6740.41

Mon Date: 1923   Responsible Agency: USCGS

To Reach: 5.1 miles E of West Yellowstone Museum, then 0.9 miles E on Riverside Road, 45 ft E of road centerline, embedded in small boulder directly W of two small roadside boulders

NOTES

PID: PY0951   Stamp: HULL   Family: N   Access: N   Ease: E

Coordinates: 44.66020745 -110.9916326   Elevation: 6701.04

Mon Date: 1987   Responsible Agency: NGS

To Reach: 5.1 miles E of West Yellowstone Museum, then 0.9 miles E on Riverside Road, on 1 ft boulder, 12 ft E of Madison River, 25 ft W of center of Riverside Rd. Across Riverside from PY0077

NOTES

PID: PY0078   Stamp: U 158 1960   Family: N   Access: N   Ease: E

Coordinates: 44.66854 -110.98188   Elevation: 6740.40

Mon Date: 1960   Responsible Agency: USCGS

To Reach: 6.9 miles E of West Yellowstone Museum, NW of the SW corner of pullout, 60 ft S of Madison River, next to a dead tree trunk.

NOTES

PID: PY0080   Stamp: A 14 RESET   Family: N   Access: N   Ease: E

Coordinates: 44.66360278 -110.96508   Elevation: 6755.15

Mon Date: 1958   Responsible Agency: USCGS

To Reach: 7.9 miles E of West Yellowstone Museum, on top of NE end of bridge over Madison River (Seven Mile Bridge), just W of Gneiss Creek Trailhead.

NOTES

PID: PY0082   Stamp: Z 13 1923 6761   Family: N   Access: N   Ease: E

Coordinates: 44.64690034 -110.93129   Elevation: 6767.02

Mon Date: 1923   Responsible Agency: USCGS

To Reach: 10.2 miles E of West Yellowstone Museum, in pullout on S side
                 of the road, 0.2 miles along pullout road, 34 ft N of pullout road
                 centerline, 100 ft NW of a sign reading "Talus".

NOTES

PID: PY0083   Stamp: S 158 1960   Family: N   Access: Y   Ease: E

Coordinates: 44.6437409 -110.9147507   Elevation: 6783.04

Mon Date: 1960   Responsible Agency: USCGS

To Reach: 11.05 miles E of West Yellowstone Museum, @ paved pullout, be-
                 tween pullout and main road, 30 ft S of main road, 25 ft NE of
                 center of pullout

NOTES

PID: PY0084   Stamp: Y 13 1923 6789   Family: N   Access: N   Ease: E

Coordinates: 44.64080476 -110.89648   Elevation: 6794.56

Mon Date: 1923   Responsible Agency: USCGS

To Reach: 12.05 miles E of West Yellowstone Museum, at pullout, in top of
                 small boulder, 23 ft NE of paved pullout road, 134 ft SW of road
                 centerline.

NOTES

PID: PY0952 Stamp: HARLEQUIN Family: N Access: N Ease: E

Coordinates: 44.63962 -110.88869   **Elevation:** 6766.64

Mon Date: 1987   **Responsible Agency:** NGS

To Reach: 12.5 miles E of West Yellowstone Museum, 87 ft S of S center edge
of Harlequin Lake Trailhead Pullout, in grass below road grade

NOTES

PID: PY0953 Stamp: WE-5 1986   Family: N Access: N Ease: M

Coordinates: 44.64008808 -110.8828682   **Elevation:** 6800.01

Mon Date: 1986   **Responsible Agency:** FHWA

To Reach: 12.8 miles E of West Yellowstone Museum, 75 ft S of road centerline, in center of island between road and "Beetle Killed and Fire
Scarred" pullout.

NOTES

PID: PY0085 Stamp: R 158 1960   Family: N Access: N Ease: E

Coordinates: 44.64168381 -110.87666   **Elevation:** 6796.36

Mon Date: 1960   **Responsible Agency:** USCGS

To Reach: 1.1 miles W of Madison Jct, @ the "Madison Elk Herd" pullout
on S side of road, 43 ft SE of road centerline, 26 NW of center of
pullout, in concrete near eastern edge of grassed area

NOTES

PID: PY0760   Stamp: 1 MDC 1975   Family: N   Access: N   Ease: M

Coordinates: 44.64543995 -110.8580492   Elevation: 6832.71

Mon Date: 1975   Responsible Agency: USGS

To Reach: At Madison Jct, 56 ft E of centerline of northbound road, 65 feet
                 N of extended center of junction, surrounded by white pipe, next
                 to 3 trees

NOTES

PID: PY0707   Stamp: D 339 1983   Family: N   Access: N   Ease: E

Coordinates: 44.64571 -110.85844   Elevation: 6837.11

Mon Date: 1983   Responsible Agency: NGS

To Reach: NW of Madison Jct, 23 ft west of "West Entrance" sign, 43 ft NW
                 of road centerline of Madison to Norris Rd, 81 ft NE of centerline
                 of West Entrance Rd. Logo cap

NOTES

Yellowstone Benchmarks
Madison Junction to Norris Junction

From Madison Junction: Reset your odometer/GPS in the middle of the intersection
From Norris Junction: Reset your odometer/GPS in the middle of the intersection

Most of the original 1923 benchmarks installed along this section of roadway have long since been destroyed, along with many installed during subsequent surveys as well. This is especially true on the southern half of the road from the old "Tanker's Curve" (at the north end of the new section) down to Madison Junction.

One of the more interesting markers is the one installed in 1960 below the north-facing retaining wall at the Norris Museum. At the time, the primary road from Norris southward ran right through the middle of the Norris Thermal Basin (the pavement that runs behind the Black Growler Steam Vent was a part of that road) and connected to the main road at the north end of Elk Park. Prior to the rerouting of the road, the area known as the "Back Basin" was behind the Norris Museum, and thus its name, even though today the basin is in front of the museum.

PID: PY1262 Stamp: PURPLE   Family: N   Access: N   Ease: D

Coordinates: 44.6598712 -110.8584208   Elevation: 8438.00

Mon Date: 1950   Responsible Agency: USCGS

To Reach: Near summit of Purple Mountain at site of old Lookout Tower.
Park at Purple Mountain trailhead, then 2.5 mile hike up to summit.

NOTES

PID: PY0087 Stamp: Q 158 1960   Family: Y   Access: Y   Ease: E

Coordinates: 44.649790 -110.84635   Elevation: 6905.58

Mon Date: 1960   Responsible Agency: USCGS

To Reach: 0.8 miles N of Madison Jct, turn into parking lot and head out onto
boardwalk. 28 ft S of Terrace Spring boardwalk at its southernmost
walkway, 70 ft N of the road centerline.

NOTES

PID: PY9922 Stamp: E   Family: Y   Access: Y   Ease: E

Coordinates: 44.650489 -110.8297   Elevation: 6901.12

Mon Date: 2002   Responsible Agency: FHWA

To Reach: 1.6 miles N of Madison Jct, benchmark is pin on the SW of the
corner of the vault toilet concrete pad at the Tuff Cliffs Picnic Area

NOTES

PID: PY9923   Stamp: STEPHY   Family: N   Access: N   Ease: E

Coordinates: 44.649154 -110.79259   Elevation: 6894.91

Mon Date: 2002   Responsible Agency: FHWA

To Reach: 3.5 miles N of Madison Jct, 7ft WSW of the W end of the stone guardrail on the S side of the road. Benchmark is pin in the guard-rail.

NOTES

PID: PY0093   Stamp: 0 9 1923 5134   Family: Y   Access: N   Ease: E

Coordinates: 44.65386 -110.77163   Elevation: 7139.57

Mon Date: 1923   Responsible Agency: USCGS

To Reach: 4.85 miles N of Madison Jct, in top of large rock at the Gibbon Falls overlook on E side of rock wall (Do not climb over the wall!)

NOTES

PID: PY0100   Stamp: G 158 1960   Family: N   Access: N   Ease: E

Coordinates: 44.67663 -110.74714   Elevation: 7305.66

Mon Date: 1960   Responsible Agency: USCGS

To Reach: 5.2 miles S of Norris Jct, 0.15 miles S of Beryl Spring, 88 ft SW of road centerline, 37 ft SW of center of pullout south of Spring, at the NE foot of steep hill, concrete post projecting 1". May be covered by dirt/debris

NOTES

PID: PY0954   Stamp: 10-11 1986   Family: N   Access: N   Ease: E

Coordinates: 44.70377 -110.74572   Elevation: 7346.45

Mon Date: 1986   Responsible Agency: FHWA

To Reach: 3.25 miles S of Norris Jct, 49 ft W of road centerline & across from pullout/service road, 20 ft W of edge of road in field on concrete pad. (NGS datasheet says "west of sign", but sign has been moved)

NOTES

PID: PY0103   Stamp: D 158 1960   Family: N   Access: N   Ease: M

Coordinates: 44.70419 -110.74506   Elevation: 7346.11

Mon Date: 1960   Responsible Agency: USCGS

To Reach: 3.25 miles S of Norris Jct, 179 ft NE and across the road from "Gibbon Meadows" sign, 129 ft NE of main road centerline, 58 ft NW of centerline of gravel pit road, SE edge of cluster of pine trees, encased in tile circle. May be overgrown by grass/trees

NOTES

PID: PY0705   Stamp: H 339 1983   Family: N   Access: N   Ease: M

Coordinates: 44.71115 -110.7391782   Elevation: 7403.09

Mon Date: 1983   Responsible Agency: NGS

To Reach: 2.65 miles S of Norris Jct, 45 ft SE & across road from northeast curb of Gibbon Rapids pullout. In 5 x 6 rock outcrop, 11 ft NE of NE corner of iron grate. May be covered by dirt

NOTES

PID: PY1126 Stamp: 2 MDC 1975   Family: N   Access: N   Ease: E

Coordinates: 44.71492 -110.73002   Elevation: 7448.38

Mon Date: 1975   Responsible Agency: USGS

To Reach: 2.0 miles S of Norris Jct, park in southernmost Elk Park Pullout, walk 165 ft SW of the SW end of pullout, 30 ft NW of road centerline, cemented into boulder in clump of trees.

NOTES

PID: PY0107 Stamp: A 158 1960   Family: Y   Access: Y   Ease: E

Coordinates: 44.726570 -110.70361   Elevation: 7572.74

Mon Date: 1960   Responsible Agency: USCGS

To Reach: At the foot of the north retaining wall surrounding Norris Museum, set in concrete.

NOTES

Yellowstone Benchmarks
Norris Junction to Canyon Junction

From Norris Junction: Reset your odometer/GPS at the intersection
From Canyon Junction: Reset your odometer/GPS at the intersection

Most of the existing benchmarks along this section of roadway are from the 1976 USGS or the 1987 NGS surveys. Though there are a handful from earlier surveys, most of the older ones were destroyed during reconstruction of this road. In addition to those along the main road, you'll find a couple along the Virginia Cascade scenic road (which was part of the original roadway between Norris and Canyon). The Virginia Cascade Road opens around late May most seasons, and typically closes after the first major snowfall in October. Some of the benchmarks along the main road are located along the power line easement that runs parallel to the roadway on the south side of the highway. If you go hunting for benchmarks along these areas, do not interfere with the electrical equipment.

PID: PY0976 | Stamp: D 365 1987   Family: N   Access: N   Ease: M

Coordinates: 44.72697 -110.69617   Elevation: 7529.74

Mon Date: 1987   Responsible Agency: NGS

To Reach: SE of Norris Jct intersection, 99 ft S of E/B lanes, & 99 ft E of S/B lanes, due S of sign for W/B traffic, in burned wooded area. Logo cap

NOTES

PID: PY0978 | Stamp: 1 MDC 1976   Family: N   Access: N   Ease: E

Coordinates: 44.72666 -110.688424   Elevation: 7490.92

Mon Date: 1976   Responsible Agency: USGS

To Reach: 0.4 miles E of Norris Jct, on S end of culvert over the Gibbon River.

NOTES

PID: PY0955 | Stamp: 10-12 1986   Family: N   Access: N   Ease: E

Coordinates: 44.72684 -110.68747   Elevation: 7495.01

Mon Date: 1986   Responsible Agency: FHWA

To Reach: 0.5 miles E of Norris Jct, E of Gibbon River Bridge, W of Norris Picnic Area Rd, 34 ft SW of Picnic Area sign, 20 ft S of road centerline.

NOTES

PID: PY0956   Stamp: F 365 1987   Family: N   Access: N   Ease: M

Coordinates: 44.72347642 -110.6771479   Elevation: 7543.43

Mon Date: 1987   Responsible Agency: NGS

To Reach: 1.05 miles E of Norris Jct, 41 ft SW of road centerline, 65 ft SE &
             across road from "Trucks Turning" sign for W/B traffic. No good
             pullout here. Logo cap.

NOTES

PID: PY0957   Stamp: 2 MDC 1976   Family: N   Access: Y   Ease: E

Coordinates: 44.71865 -110.66568   Elevation: 7605.58

Mon Date: 1976   Responsible Agency: USGS

To Reach: 1.65 miles E of Norris Jct, at entrance to Virginia Cascade Rd, just
             left of barricade, inside white PVC pipe @ ground level

NOTES

PID: PY0958   Stamp: A 367 1987   Family: N   Access: N   Ease: M

Coordinates: 44.71487 -110.6558993   Elevation: 7699.74

Mon Date: 1987   Responsible Agency: NGS

To Reach: 1.65 miles E of Norris Jct, then 0.6 miles E on Virginia Cascade
             Rd, on 2x3 rock ledge at base of rock cut, 22.6 ft N of lone guard
             post & 13.8 ft N of road centerline. Will be covered with dirt/
             pebbles

NOTES

PID: PY0140   Stamp: T 9 1925   **Family: N**   **Access: Y**   **Ease: E**

Coordinates: 44.71281 -110.64667   **Elevation: 7761.96**

Mon Date: 1925   **Responsible Agency: USCGS**

To Reach: 1.65 miles E of Norris Jct, then 1.15 miles E on Virginia Cascade Drive, N side of road in a rock between pullout for cascades & next pullout.

NOTES

PID: PY0959   Stamp: 3 MDC 1976   **Family: N**   **Access: N**   **Ease: E**

Coordinates: 44.71491244 -110.6312552   **Elevation: 7853.97**

Mon Date: 1976   **Responsible Agency: USGS**

To Reach: 3.65 miles E of Norris Jct, on culvert headwall on N side of road across from & just E of exit from Virginia Cascade Road

NOTES

PID: PY0960   Stamp: B 367 1987   **Family: N**   **Access: N**   **Ease: M**

Coordinates: 44.70961 -110.6208512   **Elevation: 7938.42**

Mon Date: 1987   **Responsible Agency: NGS**

To Reach: 4.2 miles E of Norris Jct, near center of a rock outcrop, 4 ft SW of the E end of culvert, on S side of road. Will need to park slightly E of outcrop and walk back about 150 ft

NOTES

PID: PY0961 | Stamp: 4 MDC 1976   Family: N   Access: N   Ease: E

Coordinates: 44.70798686 -110.61693   Elevation: 8031.97

Mon Date: 1987   Responsible Agency: USGS

To Reach: 4.45 miles E of Norris Jct, on slight hill 50 ft E/SE of the SE point
of the pullout on the N side of the road & 42 ft NE of the road
centerline, 30 ft N of curvy road warning sign

NOTES

PID: PY0962 | Stamp: C 367 1987   Family: N   Access: N   Ease: M

Coordinates: 44.7041352 -110.60636   Elevation: 8167.60

Mon Date: 1987   Responsible Agency: NGS

To Reach: 5.15 miles E of Norris Jct, 1.5 miles E of exit from Virginia Cascade Rd, 89 ft S of the road centerline, 3 ft E of power pole

NOTES

PID: PY0963 | Stamp: 5 MDC 1976   Family: N   Access: N   Ease: M

Coordinates: 44.70341 -110.5968178   Elevation: 8232.73

Mon Date: 1976   Responsible Agency: USGS

To Reach: 5.55 miles E of Norris Jct, in 1x4 boulder 50 ft S of road centerline across the road from west end of pullout with sign "Naturally
Reseeded by Fire..."

NOTES

PID: PY9908   Stamp: NORCAN-1   Family: N   Access: N   Ease: E

Coordinates: **44.71462 -110.5543556**   Elevation: **8121.28**

Mon Date: **1986**   Responsible Agency: **FHWA**

To Reach: 7.85 miles E of Norris Jct, 30 ft S of road centerline, on small hill, 3.5 ft from metal pole next to a lone tree.

NOTES

PID: PY0964   Stamp: 6 MDC 1976   Family: N   Access: N   Ease: M

Coordinates: **44.70377 -110.58028**   Elevation: **8225.25**

Mon Date: **1976**   Responsible Agency: **USGS**

To Reach: 5.35 miles W of Canyon Jct, 100 ft S of road centerline in 2x3 boulder, 91 ft E of power pole

NOTES

PID: PY0141   Stamp: V 9 1923   Family: N   Access: N   Ease: M

Coordinates: **44.70813 -110.5689**   Elevation: **8187.47**

Mon Date: **1923**   Responsible Agency: **USCGS**

To Reach: 4.6 miles W of Canyon Jct, at small pullout on S side of road, 40 ft W of ravine, 61 ft south of road centerline in a rock, 7 ft below road surface level

NOTES

PID: PY0968   Stamp: E 367 1987   Family: N   Access: N   Ease: M

Coordinates: 44.73128 -110.5227600   Elevation: 8038.38

Mon Date: 1987   Responsible Agency: NGS

To Reach: 1.6 miles W of Canyon Jct, 35 ft W of road centerline, 43 ft S of storm drain (hard to see), 2 ft above road surface level in woods. Logo cap (damaged)

NOTES

PID: PY0970   Stamp: LC 38 1977   Family: N   Access: N   Ease: E

Coordinates: 44.73473 -110.51453   Elevation: 7918.02

Mon Date: 1977   Responsible Agency: NPS

To Reach: 1.05 miles W of Canyon Jct, @ very small pullout on N side of road, 66 ft N of road centerline, next to white witness post.

NOTES

PID: PY0971   Stamp: 10-26 1986   Family: N   Access: N   Ease: E

Coordinates: 44.73544 -110.50366   Elevation: 7892.10

Mon Date: 1986   Responsible Agency: FHWA

To Reach: 0.4 miles W of Canyon Jct, 77 ft W of Cascade Creek trail, 33 ft N of curb of turnout.

NOTES

| PID: PY0972 | Stamp: D 367 1987 | Family: N | Access: N | Ease: E |

Coordinates: 44.73622 -110.49877   **Elevation:** 7890.12

Mon Date: 1987   **Responsible Agency:** NGS

To Reach: 0.25 miles W of Canyon Jct, 105 feet W of Canyon Govt Area
Service Rd, 57 ft N of road centerline. Logo cap

NOTES

Yellowstone Benchmarks
Norris Junction to Mammoth Hot Springs

From Norris Junction: Reset your odometer/GPS at the intersection
From Mammoth Hot Springs: Reset your odometer/GPS in front of the Mammoth Post Office.

The vast majority of benchmarks along this section of roadway are from the 1960 USCGS survey done in the aftermath of the Hebgen Lake earthquake. There are a small handful from the USGS surveys in the mid-1970s, as well as a couple of the old, original markers from the 1923 USCGS surveys. A couple of good examples of these include the pedestal-based benchmarks at Roaring Mountain and Apollinaris Spring. The marker at Obsidian Cliff is also from 1923.

One of the more unique markers in the park can be found on the small hill just south of the entrance to the Mammoth Corral. It is a Department of Interior marker (PY0137) whose exact installation date is unknown. It may have been installed around the time the original Mammoth Lodge was constructed in 1917. The Lodge and its cabins occupied the vast space you see to the immediate north of the Corral. If you walk out into the grassy area here, you'll see bits and pieces of the old foundations from some of the buildings that were here. The undocumented NPS marker 20 feet to the south of this was installed during the construction of Mammoth's new water system in the late 1970s.

PID: PY0110   Stamp: Z 157 1960   Family: N   Access: N   Ease: E

Coordinates: 44.7381496 -110.6988793   Elevation: 7478.11

Mon Date: 1960   Responsible Agency: USCGS

To Reach: 0.7 miles N of Norris Jct, on NW end of the bridge, in sidewalk.

NOTES

PID: PY0113   Stamp: X 157 1960   Family: N   Access: N   Ease: E

Coordinates: 44.7533574 -110.72467   Elevation: 7523.13

Mon Date: 1960   Responsible Agency: USCGS

To Reach: 2.65 N of Norris Jct, 0.1 miles N of Frying Pan Springs, 120 ft SE of Nymph Lake pullout, on W side of highway, on crest of a barren bench, in a concrete pad. Walk around south of thermal area.

NOTES

PID: PY0115   Stamp: V 157 1960   Family: N   Access: N   Ease: M

Coordinates: 44.77299 -110.73417   Elevation: 7556.58

Mon Date: 1960   Responsible Agency: USCGS

To Reach: 4.15 miles N of Norris Jct, 216 ft N/NW of pullout for South Twin Lake on W side of road, 44 ft SW of road centerline, on small rocky knoll.

NOTES

PID: PY0116   Stamp: F 9 1923 7575   Family: Y   Access: Y   Ease: E

Coordinates: 44.78086 -110.7408   Elevation: 7580.39

Mon Date: 1923   Responsible Agency: USCGS

To Reach: 4.85 miles N of Norris Jct, @ S end of pullout for Roaring Moun-
               tain, 4 ft S of sign, on concrete pedestal.

NOTES

PID: PY0117   Stamp: U 157 1960   Family: N   Access: N   Ease: E

Coordinates: 44.78778 -110.73906   Elevation: 7530.17

Mon Date: 1960   Responsible Agency: USCGS

To Reach: 5.35 miles N of Norris Jct, 0.5 miles N of Roaring Mountain, on W
               side of highway at a pullout for a dirt trail that leads to a thermal
               area, 77 ft W of road centerline, 45 ft W of edge of parking area

NOTES

PID: PY0119   Stamp: T 157 1960   Family: N   Access: N   Ease: M

Coordinates: 44.79865 -110.74491   Elevation: 7443.96

Mon Date: 1960   Responsible Agency: USCGS

To Reach: 6.25 miles N of Norris Jct, on E side of road from "Grizzly Lake"
               pullout, on SW flank of a hill, in rock outcrop, 8.5 ft above road
               surface

NOTES

PID: PY0120   Stamp: S 157 1960   Family: N   Access: N   Ease: M

Coordinates: 44.81108 -110.73151   Elevation: 7393.17

Mon Date: 1960   Responsible Agency: USCGS

To Reach: 7.45 miles N of Norris Jct, NW of intersection, 77 ft W of highway
                centerline, 32 ft N of Beaver Lake Picnic Area entrance road, 75 ft
                ESE of Vault Toilet. May be covered by dirt/debris

NOTES

PID: PY0121   Stamp: D 9 1923 7382   Family: N   Access: N   Ease: M

Coordinates: 44.820599 -110.727771   Elevation: 7387.79

Mon Date: 1923   Responsible Agency: USCGS

To Reach: 8.2 miles N of Norris Jct, 0.2 miles S of Obsidian Creek, @ SW
                base of Obsidian Cliff, in top of obsidian boulder projecting 6"
                above surface under a small tree, 21.5 ft E of road centerline. Park
                at exhibit and walk S approx .25 mile. Watch out for traffic while
                crossing road.

NOTES

PID: PY1266   Stamp: HOLMES 1950   Family: N   Access: N   Ease: D

Coordinates: 44.8187755 -110.8557482   Elevation: 10340.00

Mon Date: 1950   Responsible Agency: USCGS

To Reach: 84 ft N of Mt. Holmes Fire Lookout. Park at Mt. Holmes Trail-
                head and hike to summit (generally an overnight hike; 10 miles
                each way)

NOTES

PID: PY0122   **Stamp: R 157 1960**   **Family: N**   **Access: N**   **Ease: E**

Coordinates: 44.83291 -110.72887   **Elevation: 7363.88**

Mon Date: 1960   **Responsible Agency: USCGS**

To Reach: 9.05 miles N of Norris Jct, 0.6 miles N of Obsidian Cliff interpretive exhibit, on W side of highway across from gravel pullout, S of pullout, in 3x5 ft boulder,

NOTES

PID: PY0123   **Stamp: C 9 1923 7337**   **Family: Y**   **Access: N**   **Ease: E**

Coordinates: 44.8427427 -110.7336   **Elevation: 7342.60**

Mon Date: 1923   **Responsible Agency: USCGS**

To Reach: 9.8 miles N of Norris Jct, 29 ft N/NW of northernmost steps leading to Apollinaris Springs on E side of road, 28 ft from road centerline, mounted in 1 ft high concrete post

NOTES

PID: PY0124   **Stamp: Q 157 1960**   **Family: N**   **Access: N**   **Ease: E**

Coordinates: 44.85077 -110.73653   **Elevation: 7313.94**

Mon Date: 1960   **Responsible Agency: USCGS**

To Reach: 10.8 miles S of Mammoth Post Office, 14ft NW of Moose Exhibit sign (behind you to the right, as you read the sign), in top of obsidian boulder in clump of bushes

NOTES

PID: PY0125 Stamp: P 157 1960   Family: N   Access: Y   Ease: E

Coordinates: 44.8613141 -110.736895057   Elevation: 7302.16

Mon Date: 1960   Responsible Agency: USCGS

To Reach: 10.0 miles S of Mammoth Post Office, at SW edge of Moose Flat pullout (has a vault toilet), on social trail off south end of parking area, in a white PVC pipe sticking up 5" from the surface.

NOTES

PID: PY0126 Stamp: N 157 1960   Family: N   Access: Y   Ease: E

Coordinates: 44.8770027 -110.73659   Elevation: 7299.20

Mon Date: 1960   Responsible Agency: USCGS

To Reach: 8.95 miles S of Mammoth Post Office, S of Indian Creek Campground in pullout on east side of road just south of a small unnamed lake on the east side. 25 ft from the northeast corner of the pullout pavement

NOTES

PID: PY0127 Stamp: M 157 1960   Family: N   Access: Y   Ease: E

Coordinates: 44.88824 -110.73254   Elevation: 7291.18

Mon Date: 1960   Responsible Agency: USCGS

To Reach: 8.1 miles S of Mammoth Post Office, NE of stop sign at entrance to Sheepeater Cliff Drive

NOTES

PID: PY9902 Stamp: SLF 6 1976   Family: N   Access: Y   Ease: E

Coordinates: 44.89408 -110.7342   Elevation: 7432.48

Mon Date: 1976   Responsible Agency: NPS

To Reach: 7.7 miles S of Mammoth Post Office, NW of intersection of Grand
              Loop Road and Mammoth Aqueduct Service Road, 1.5 meters W
              of "Service Road" sign.

NOTES

PID: PY0128 Stamp: L 157 1960   Family: N   Access: Y   Ease: E

Coordinates: 44.894161 -110.734233   Elevation: 7333.27

Mon Date: 1960   Responsible Agency: USCGS

To Reach: 7.7 miles S of Mammoth Post Office, NW of intersection of Grand
              Loop Road & Mammoth Aqueduct Service Road, 62 feet W/NW
              of intersection center. 3 feet behind the "Service Road" sign. May
              be covered by dirt/debris

NOTES

PID: PY0129 Stamp: K 157 1960   Family: N   Access: N   Ease: M

Coordinates: 44.906469 -110.732642   Elevation: 7300.99

Mon Date: 1960   Responsible Agency: USCGS

To Reach: 6.8 miles S of Mammoth Post Office, 2000 ft S of Swan Lake, on
              rock outcropping S of Swan Lake Flat on W side of road, 160 ft N
              of pullout on E side of road, 44 ft W of road centerline

NOTES

PID: PY0130   Stamp: J 157 1960   Family: N   Access: N   Ease: E

Coordinates: 44.92049 -110.73127   Elevation: 7277.76

Mon Date: 1960   Responsible Agency: USCGS

To Reach: 5.85 miles S of Mammoth Post Office, 54 ft E of highway center-
              line @ Gallatin Range Turnout

NOTES

PID: PY0977   Stamp: 10-17 1986   Family: N   Access: N   Ease: E

Coordinates: 44.93155 -110.72877   Elevation: 7275.58

Mon Date: 1986   Responsible Agency: FHWA

To Reach: 4.95 miles S of Mammoth Post Office, 117 ft NE of the N end of
              the Glen Creek Trailhead Stock pullout on the west side of road,
              60 ft E of road centerline. Marker has varnish on it, damaged

NOTES

PID: PY0702   Stamp: 3 MDC 1975   Family: N   Access: N   Ease: E

Coordinates: 44.9333328 -110.727047434   Elevation: 7262.30

Mon Date: 1975   Responsible Agency: USGS

To Reach: 4.8 miles S of Mammoth Post Office @ Rustic Falls. On east stone
              guard rail at the end (or first if you're driving north), 42 ft E of road
              centerline. Stop at top Rustic Falls pullout and walk back about 50
              yards – be careful of oncoming traffic.

NOTES

| PID: PY1259 | Stamp: BUNSEN 8564 | Family: N | Access: N | Ease: D |

Coordinates: 44.93165 -110.70617   **Elevation:** 8568.00

Mon Date: 1955   **Responsible Agency:** USGS

To Reach: Near summit of Bunsen Peak, on the SE and lowest of the three rocky points, site of old fire lookout, 150 ft SW of radio tower. Full stamp reads: 1955 8564 BUNSEN

NOTES

| PID: PY0133 | Stamp: G 157 1960 | Family: N | Access: N | Ease: E |

Coordinates: 44.94679 -110.71449   **Elevation:** 7003.47

Mon Date: 1960   **Responsible Agency:** USCGS

To Reach: 3.5 miles S of Mammoth Post Office, @ Cathedral Rock Pullout in sharp curve just below Silver Gate, in reddish rock outcrop against the wall of rock on the west end of the pullout.

NOTES

| PID: PY0134 | Stamp: F 157 1960 | Family: N | Access: N | Ease: M |

Coordinates: 44.95752 -110.7121   **Elevation:** 6809.50

Mon Date: 1960   **Responsible Agency:** USCGS

To Reach: 2.8 miles S of Mammoth Post Office, in 3x3 white rock outcrop on W side of road, 38 ft N of the N edge of unpaved pullout.

NOTES

PID: PY0701	Stamp: A 339 1983	Family: N	Access: N	Ease: E

Coordinates: 44.9656 -110.70808   **Elevation:** 6617.29

Mon Date: 1983   **Responsible Agency:** NGS

To Reach: On west side of Upper Terrace Drive just after the northerly (right-hand) turn off the main roadway. Marker is on top of white rock about three feet above the roadway next to a tree.

NOTES

PID: PY0974	Stamp: 4 MDC 1975	Family: N	Access: N	Ease: M

Coordinates: 44.96655 -110.70625   **Elevation:** 6580.36

Mon Date: 1975   **Responsible Agency:** USGS

To Reach: 2.05 miles S of Mammoth Post Office, at apex inside the curve just north of Upper Terrace Drive lot, 58 ft east of road centerline, 37 ft SE of E end of pullout. Short hike up hill east of several brown fiberglass reflective markers

NOTES

PID: PY0136	Stamp: D 157 1960	Family: N	Access: N	Ease: M

Coordinates: 44.95883 -110.702999762   **Elevation:** 6453.19

Mon Date: 1960   **Responsible Agency:** USCGS

To Reach: 1.4 miles S of Mammoth Post Office, SE of YACC Road intersection with Grand Loop Road, 66 ft S of main road centerline, SW edge of a 7 x 8 ft rock outcrop on boulder behind tree, 16 ft E of "Trail" sign.

NOTES

PID: PY0137   **Stamp: MS LINE STA**   **Family: N**   **Access: N**   **Ease: E**

Coordinates: 44.96582 -110.70113   **Elevation: 6363.46**

Mon Date: Unknown   **Responsible Agency: NPS**

To Reach: 0.9 miles S of Mammoth Post Office, S of RV parking area at entrance to Mammoth Corrals near road, on hill 3 ft above roadway. NGS datasheet lists stamp as "DI 19."

NOTES

PID: PY9907   **Stamp: C 1977**   **Family: N**   **Access: N**   **Ease: E**

Coordinates: 44.96574 -110.70111   **Elevation: 6379.00**

Mon Date: 1977   **Responsible Agency: NPS**

To Reach: 0.9 miles S of Mammoth Post Office, S of RV parking area at entrance to Mammoth corrals near road, on hill 4 ft above roadway, 20 ft S of PY0137

NOTES

PID: PY0138   **Stamp: C 157 1960**   **Family: N**   **Access: N**   **Ease: E**

Coordinates: 44.97006 -110.70192   **Elevation: 6355.69**

Mon Date: 1960   **Responsible Agency: USCGS**

To Reach: 0.7 miles S of Mammoth Post Office, across from the terraces, NE of parking area's north entrance/exit, 45 ft E of road centerline

NOTES

Yellowstone Benchmarks
U. S. Highway 191

From the North: Reset your odometer/GPS at the north entrance sign
From the South: Reset your odometer/GPS at the intersection of US 191 (Canyon Street) and Yellowstone Avenue in front of the West Yellowstone Museum

There are a tremendous number of benchmarks along US191 from West Yellowstone north through the park. This list contains only a handful that are found within the park's borders along this stretch of roadway. There are numerous markers that were installed by the Montana Highway Commission at some point. They can be seen on white posts a few yards to the west of the roadway. Many of these markers do not appear in the NGS database, however, and only a couple are provided in this book, including the one at the park's entrance sign on the north end of US191.

Most of the non-Montana benchmarks are from either the original 1934 USCGS leveling survey or the 1960 survey performed in the aftermath of the Hebgen Lake earthquake. There are a few markers from the 1931 survey undertaken by the General Land Office (GLO) to be found around these parts as well. Future editions of this book will have further details on these.

PID: QX9901 | Stamp: 6699.55   Family: Y   Access: Y   Ease: E

Coordinates: 45.0541 -111.15541   Elevation: 6699.55

Mon Date: Unknown   Responsible Agency: MHC

To Reach: On pedestal in front of northern YNP entrance sign on US191. This is NOT marker QX0314, which can be found across the street.

NOTES

PID: QX0317 | Stamp: M 161 1960   Family: N   Access: N   Ease: M

Coordinates: 45.03952 -111.12112   Elevation: 6780.86

Mon Date: 1960   Responsible Agency: USCGS

To Reach: 6.9 miles S of 320 Ranch Rd, in top of rock 53 ft N of road centerline.

NOTES

PID: PY0164 | Stamp: R 161 1960   Family: N   Access: N   Ease: E

Coordinates: 44.96386 -111.07522   Elevation: 7066.34

Mon Date: 1960   Responsible Agency: USCGS

To Reach: 23.2 miles N of West Yellowstone Museum, 0.6 miles S of bridge over Gallatin River, in flat rock, 56 ft NE of road centerline, next to orange fiberglass survey marker post.

NOTES

PID: PY0176   Stamp: ELEV 6924.77   Family: N   Access: N   Ease: M

Coordinates: 44.856643 -111.055939   Elevation: 6930.92

Mon Date: Unknown   Responsible Agency: MHC

To Reach: 15.15 miles N of West Yellowstone West Yellowstone Museum on US191, 0.1 miles NE of bridge crossing Grayling Creek, 77 ft NW of road centerline, in top of 3 ft tall concrete post

NOTES

PID: PY0177   Stamp: W 161 1960   Family: N   Access: N   Ease: E

Coordinates: 44.85012 -111.06628   Elevation: 6893.74

Mon Date: 1960   Responsible Agency: USCGS

To Reach: 14.45 miles N of West Yellowstone West Yellowstone Museum on US191, 50 ft E of road centerline, in top of large rounded boulder

NOTES

Yellowstone Benchmarks
Miscellaneous Benchmarks

The benchmarks found in this section are scattered around the park and generally not located along one of the major roadways. These include markers found on side roads in the Canyon, Fountain Flat, and Reese Creek areas, as well as a marker located on the hill behind the Mammoth Hotel. The single marker located in the Bechler area is also included in this list.

PID: QX0102   Stamp: F 33 1923 5178   Family: N   Access: N   Ease: M

Coordinates: 45.05354 -110.76146   Elevation: 5182.90

Mon Date: 1923   Responsible Agency: USCGS

To Reach: 3.2 miles NW of Gardiner along old railroad bed (the dirt road running behind the Heritage and Research Center), 0.6 miles NW of Stephen's Creek Rd, at curve in road, in the SW culvert headwall.

NOTES

PID: PY1258   Stamp: F Mammoth   Family: N   Access: N   Ease: D

Coordinates: 44.98187 -110.70459   Elevation: 6538.00

Mon Date: 1951   Responsible Agency: USGS

To Reach: 0.2 miles toward Gardiner on Old Gardiner High Rd (dirt), then 0.35 miles S on Elk Park Service Road, then 0.15 miles cross country to top of knoll. Set in rock outcrop NW of old cemetery.

NOTES

PID: PY0973   Stamp: 11 MDC 1976   Family: N   Access: N   Ease: E

Coordinates: 44.73635 -110.4919771   Elevation: 7921.90

Mon Date: 1976   Responsible Agency: USGS

To Reach: NE of Canyon Junction, 81 ft E of the east face of the Canyon Service Station, 6 ft above road surface level in dome shaped boulder

NOTES

PID: PY0835   Stamp: 22 MDC 1976   Family: N   Access: Y   Ease: E

Coordinates: 44.70811 -110.50296   Elevation: 7702.94

Mon Date: 1976   Responsible Agency: USGS

To Reach: West end of Chittenden Bridge on South Rim Drive south of
             Canyon Village, on the south walkway

NOTES

PID: PY9905   Stamp: Flynn Co Inc   Family: N   Access: Y   Ease: M

Coordinates: 44.5622 -110.83852   Elevation: 7226.00

Mon Date: 1984   Responsible Agency: Private

To Reach: 0.4 miles S of Ojo Caliente Spring parking lot, SE abutment on
             Bridge over Firehole River on Fountain Flat Road, south of Ojo
             Caliente Spring

NOTES

PID: PY9904   Stamp: (Blank)   Family: N   Access: Y   Ease: M

Coordinates: 44.56245 -110.83838   Elevation: 7226.00

Mon Date: 1986   Responsible Agency: FHWA

To Reach: 0.4 miles S of Ojo Caliente Spring parking lot, NE abutment on
             bridge over Firehole River on Fountain Flat Road, south of Ojo
             Caliente Spring

NOTES

| PID: PY1269 | Stamp: BECHLER | Family: N | Access: N | Ease: E |

Coordinates: 44.1493126 -111.0456353   **Elevation:** 6424.00

Mon Date: 1950   **Responsible Agency:** USCGS

To Reach: Located in horse corral pen at the Bechler Ranger Station, 15 ft from corral fence, & 15 ft from grazing pen fence. May be covered by dirt or debris. Check with ranger station before entering corral.

NOTES

Part IV
Appendices

- Appendix 1: Accessible Benchmarks
- Appendix 2: Family-Friendly Benchmarks
- Appendix 3: Accessing the Book's Website
- Appendix 4: Recommended Reading
- Appendix 5: References

Appendix 1
Accessible Benchmarks

The following benchmarks are accessible to those in wheelchairs. This means that an individual in a wheelchair can get close enough to the marker to verify its identity, and can do so without jeopardizing his/her safety and without interfering with vehicular traffic flow. Though most are very close to the roadway, some may require a small travel down paved or packed gravel road. Please refer to the relevant lists for specific details on how to locate each of these.

North Entrance Road
PY9901   PY9906   PY0160

Northeast Entrance Road
QX0622

Tower Junction to Canyon Junction
PY0027   PY0984   PY0991

Canyon Junction to Fishing Bridge Junction
PY0855   PY0860   PY0864

East Entrance Road
PY0879   PY0887   PY0036

Fishing Bridge Junction to West Thumb Junction
PY0949   PY0948   PY0948A
PY0948B   PY0010   PY0947
PY9909

South Entrance Road
PY0071   PY9914   PY0804
PY0803

West Thumb Junction to Old Faithful
PY0048   PY0780

Old Faithful to Madison Junction
PY9903   PY0775   PY0148
PY0146   PY0145

West Entrance Road
PY0083

Madison Junction to Norris Junction
PY0107	PY0087	PY9922

Norris Junction to Canyon Junction
PY0957	PY0140

Norris Junction to Mammoth Hot Springs
PY0116	PY0125	PY0126
PY0127	PY9902	PY0128

U. S. Highway 191
PY9921

Fountain Flat Road (See MISC Page)
PY9905	PY9904

South Rim Drive (See MISC Page)
PY0835

Appendix 2
Family-Friendly Benchmarks

The following benchmarks are "Family Friendly." This means they're located at or in close proximity to major developments, features, or other points of interest. They're easy to find and therefore suitable for hunting by a family with small children. Notations in parentheses indicate the page number for the marker's entry in the lists.

North Entrance Road
QX0584: Next to the Roosevelt Arch. (NER-2)
QX0585: Behind the interpretive sign at the Northern Range turnout. (NER-2)
PY0160: In front of the Albright Visitor Center. (NER-5)

Tower Junction to Canyon Junction
PY0981: Across the road from the Calcite Springs Overlook. (TJ-CJ-2)
PY1215: At the summit of Mt. Washburn. (TJ-CJ-4)
CQ7584: At the summit of Mt. Washburn. (TJ-CJ-5)
CQ7585: At the summit of Mt. Washburn. (TJ-CJ-5)
PY0024: At the terminus of Chittenden Road on Mt. Washburn. (TJ-CJ-5)

Canyon Junction to Fishing Bridge Junction
PY0855: Next to the Hayden Valley interpretive sign. (CJ-FB-9)

Fishing Bridge to West Thumb
PY0949: Large granite block in front of the Lake Lodge. (FB-WT-2)
PY9918: Behind the old Lake Service Station near the gravesites. (FB-WT-3)
PY0010: In the woods across the street from the Lake Hotel. (FB-WT-3)
PY0947: In the sand adjacent to the dock in front of the Lake Hotel. (FB-WT-4)
PY9909: On the bridge abutment behind the old Lake Boathouse. (FB-WT-4)

South Entrance Road
PY0814: On the bridge walkway at Lewis Falls. (SER-4)
PY0813: On the bridge walkway at Lewis Falls. (SER-5)

West Thumb to Old Faithful
PY0053: On the southeast side of Isa Lake @ the Continental Divide. (WT-OF-4)
PY0048: At Kepler Cascade Pullout. (WT-OF-6)

Old Faithful to Madison Junction

PY9903: In the woods across the parking lot from the O. F. Lodge. (OF-MD-2)

PY0148: On the old iron bridge at the Fairy Falls Trailhead. (OF-MD-4)

PY0145: Junction of Firehole Canyon Road & Grand Loop Road. (OF-MD-7)

Madison Junction to Norris Junction

PY0087: S of the southernmost section of boardwalk @ Terrace Spring. (MD-NJ-2)

PY9922: At the vault toilet at the Tuff Cliff Picnic Area. (MD-NJ-2)

PY0093: At the Gibbon Falls Overlook. (MD-NJ-3)

PY0107: At the foot of the retaining wall on N side of Norris Museum. (MD-NJ-5)

Norris Junction to Mammoth Hot Springs

PY0116: At the Roaring Mountain exhibit. (NJ-MHS-3)

PY0123: At northern steps to Apollinaris Spring exhibit. (NJ-MHS-5)

U. S. Highway 191

QX9901: At the northern Yellowstone National Park entrance sign. (US191-3)

Appendix 3
Accessing the Book's Website

Accompanying this book is a web site created specifically to provide additional and supportive information about the benchmarks located in Yellowstone National Park. The web site is at www.yellowstonebenchmarks.com. To gain access to the additional information, you'll need a password. The passwords will be based on information contained in this book.

Information on the web site includes:

- Individual and contextual photographs of the markers listed in this book, along with any additional information that might aid you in locating the markers.
- Links to the NGS Datasheets and the Geocaching web pages for the markers listed in this book.
- GPX files of the markers identified in the lists in this book, plus a GPX file of other markers from the NGS database that were not included in this book.
- Corrections and additions to information contained within the book. Sign up for periodic newsletters and e-mails with updates about the book.
- There's also a contact form you can use to report errors, or to provide information about markers you may have found that have not been included in the book.

APPENDIX 4
RECOMMENDED READING

Geocaching

Geocaching for Dummies. Joel McNamara, 2004. This is an excellent introduction to the game/sport of geocaching if you're unfamiliar with it.

GPS Use

GPS For Dummies. Joel McNamara, 2008. This is an excellent introduction to the use of GPS devices, including their limitations.

Hiking

Yellowstone Trails: A Hiking Guide, 30th Edition. Mark and Joy Sellers Marschall, 2008. Published by the Yellowstone Association, this is the slightly better of the two hiking books I recommend. The spiral-bound version has a fold out map in the back of it, and both versions have an index of the trails, which is why I recommend it over the Schneider book.

Hiking Yellowstone National Park, 2nd Edition. Bill Schneider, 2003. Both Bill's book and the one above are excellent references for the 1000+ miles of trails in Yellowstone. You can't go wrong with either book.

You'll also want to read the park's *Backcountry Trip Planner*, which can be found on the park's web site at http://www.nps.gov/yell.

Miscellaneous

Yellowstone Place Names, Second Edition, Revised. Lee H. Whittlsey, 2006. This book may be tough to find as it is no longer being published. It's an excellent source of information about why features and places throughout the park have the names they do.

APPENDIX 5
REFERENCES

Chittenden, Hiram M. *Yellowstone National Park: Historical and Descriptive*, 5th ed., Revised by Eleanor Chittenden Cress and Isabelle F. Story. Stanford, CA: Stanford University Press, 1949.

Culpin, Mary Shivers, *The History of the Construction of the Road System in Yellowstone National Park, 1872-1966: Historic Resource Study, Part I.* National Park Service, Denver, 1994.

Dzurisin, Daniel, K. M. Yamashita, and D. J. Johnson, *Preliminary Results of Precise Leveling and Trilateration Surveys in Yellowstone National Park, Wyoming, 1985.* USGS Open File Report 86-265-B, 1985.

Floyd, Lt. Richard P. *NOAA Manual NOS NGS 1: Geodetic Bench Marks*, National Geodetic Survey. September, 1978.

Leigh, CDR (Ret) George E., *Bottles, Pots, and Pans? Marking the Surveys of the U.S. Coast and Geodetic Survey and NOAA.* National Oceanic and Atmospheric Administration, Unknown Date. http://www.ngs.noaa.gov/web/about_ngs/history/Survey_Mark_Art.pdf

National Oceanic and Atmospheric Administration, *NOAA Manual NOS NGS 1: Geodetic Benchmarks*, National Geodetic Survey, 1978.

Pelton, J. R., and R. B. Smith, "Contemporary Vertical Surface Displacements in Yellowstone National Park," *Journal of Geophysical Research* 87, No. B4, April, 1982: 2745-2761.

Puskas, C. M., R. B. Smith, C. M. Meertens, and W. L. Chang, "Crustal Deformation of the Yellowstone-Snake River Plain Volcanic System: Campaign and continuous GPS observations, 1987-2004," *Journal of Geophysical Research* 112, No. B03401, 2007. doi:10.1029/2006JB004325

Richardson, James. *Wonders of the Yellowstone Region in the Rocky Mountains, Being a Description of its Geysers, Hot-Springs, Grand Canyon, Waterfalls, Lake, and Surrounding Scenery, Explored in 1870-1871.* London: Blackie and Son, 1874.

Smith, Curtis L. *Setting a NGS 3-D Monument*, National Geodetic Survey, July, 1996.

Stoopes, Gary, and K. M. Yamashita, *Preliminary Results of a Precise Leveling Survey in Yellowstone National Park, Wyoming, September 1986.* USGS Open File Report 88-24, 1988.

U. S. Coast and Geodetic Survey, *Report of the Superintendent of the U. S. Coast and Geodetic Survey Showing the Progress of the Work During the Fiscal Year Ending with June, 1892.* Washington, DC: U. S. Government Printing Office, 1893.

U. S. Geological Survey, *Twenty First Annual Report of the U. S. Geological Survey to the Secretary of the Interior, 1899-1900., Part I.* Washington, DC: U.S. Government Printing Office, 1900.

Index of PIDs

PY0857 CJ-FB-10
PY0860 CJ-FB-10
PY0863 CJ-FB-10
PY0864 CJ-FB-11
PY0865 CJ-FB-11
PY0866 CJ-FB-12
PY0867 CJ-FB-12
PY0872 CJ-FB-13
PY0874 EER-2
PY0875 CJ-FB-5
PY0876 EER-2
PY0877 EER-3
PY0878 EER-3
PY0879 EER-3
PY0880 EER-4
PY0881 EER-4
PY0882 EER-5
PY0887 EER-5
PY0901 CJ-FB-7
PY0931 FB-WT-7
PY0933 FB-WT-7
PY0934 FB-WT-7
PY0935 FB-WT-6
PY0941 FB-WT-6
PY0943 FB-WT-5
PY0945 FB-WT-5
PY0946 FB-WT-4
PY0947 FB-WT-4
PY0948 FB-WT-2
PY0949 FB-WT-2
PY0950 WER-2
PY0951 WER-5
PY0952 WER-7
PY0953 WER-7
PY0954 MD-NJ-4
PY0955 NJ-CJ-2
PY0956 NJ-CJ-3
PY0957 NJ-CJ-3
PY0958 NJ-CJ-3
PY0959 NJ-CJ-4
PY0960 NJ-CJ-4
PY0961 NJ-CJ-5
PY0962 NJ-CJ-5
PY0963 NJ-CJ-5
PY0964 NJ-CJ-6
PY0968 NJ-CJ-7
PY0970 NJ-CJ-7
PY0971 NJ-CJ-7
PY0972 NJ-CJ-8
PY0973 MISC-2
PY0974 NJ-MHS-10
PY0976 NJ-CJ-2
PY0977 NJ-MHS-8
PY0978 NJ-CJ-2
PY0979 TJ-CJ-2
PY0981 TJ-CJ-2

PY0982 TJ-CJ-2
PY0984 TJ-CJ-3
PY0987 TJ-CJ-3
PY0988 TJ-CJ-4
PY0991 TJ-CJ-4
PY1002 TJ-CJ-6
PY1006 TJ-CJ-6
PY1008 MHS-TJ-2
PY1009 MHS-TJ-2
PY1010 MHS-TJ-2
PY1015 MHS-TJ-3
PY1016 MHS-TJ-4
PY1017 MHS-TJ-4
PY1018 MHS-TJ-4
PY1020 MHS-TJ-5
PY1022 MHS-TJ-5
PY1023 MHS-TJ-6
PY1028 MHS-TJ-6
PY1029 MHS-TJ-7
PY1035 MHS-TJ-7
PY1036 NEER-2
PY1037 NEER-2
PY1038 NEER-2
PY1039 NEER-3
PY1043 NEER-3
PY1049 NEER-4
PY1051 NEER-4
PY1052 NEER-5
PY1053 NEER-5
PY1055 NEER-5
PY1058 NEER-6
PY1059 NEER-6
PY1060 NEER-6
PY1063 NEER-7
PY1067 NEER-7
PY1069 NEER-7
PY1071 NEER-8
PY1072 NEER-8
PY1074 NEER-8
PY1077 NEER-3
PY1078 NEER-4
PY1125 NEER-9
PY1126 MD-NJ-5
PY1129 SER-8
PY1131 SER-8
PY1132 SER-9
PY1135 WT-OF-3
PY1142 WT-OF-7
PY1210 EER-4
PY1211 EER-6
PY1215 TJ-CJ-4
PY1238 SER-7
PY1255 TJ-CJ-7
PY1258 MISC-2
PY1259 NJ-MHS-9
PY1262 MD-NJ-2

PY1264 OF-MD-4
PY1266 NJ-MHS-4
PY1269 MISC-4
PY1278 WT-OF-3
PY9902 NJ-MHS-7
PY9903 OF-MD-2
PY9904 MISC-3
PY9905 MISC-3
PY9906 NER-3
PY9907 NJ-MHS-11
PY9908 NJ-CJ-6
PY9909 FB-WT-4
PY9910 WT-OF-2
PY9911 FB-WT-8
PY9912 EER-5
PY9913 FB-WT-5
PY9914 SER-2
PY9915 TJ-CJ-6
PY9916 CJ-FB-3
PY9917 CJ-FB-3
PY9918 FB-WT-3
PY9919 CJ-FB-12
PY9920 OF-MD-3
PY9922 MD-NJ-2
PY9923 MD-NJ-3
PY9924 SER-5

QX0102 MISC-2
QX0116 NER-3
QX0314 US191-2
QX0317 US191-2
QX0584 NER-2
QX0585 NER-2
QX0622 NEER-9
QX9901 US191-2
QX9902 NER-2

www.ingramcontent.com/pod-product-compliance
Lightning Source LLC
Chambersburg PA
CBHW021231090426
42740CB00006B/481